Collins

KS3 Science Progress Tests

For KS3 in England and Wales

and for Third Level in Scotland

Authors:
Heidi Foxford, Aidan Gill,

Dorothy Warren

William Collins' dream of knowledge for all began with the publication of his first book in 1819. A self-educated mill worker, he not only enriched millions of lives, but also founded a flourishing publishing house. Today, staying true to this spirit, Collins books are packed with inspiration, innovation and practical expertise. They place you at the centre of a world of possibility and give you exactly what you need to explore it.

Collins. Freedom to teach.

Published by Collins
An imprint of HarperCollins*Publishers*
The News Building, 1 London Bridge Street, London, SE1 9GF, UK

HarperCollins Publishers
1st Floor, Watermarque Building, Ringsend Road, Dublin 4, Ireland

Browse the complete Collins catalogue at
www.collins.co.uk

© HarperCollins*Publishers* Limited 2019

10 9 8 7 6 5 4 3 2 1

ISBN 978-0-00-833369-0

British Library Cataloguing-in-Publication Data
A catalogue record for this publication is available from the British Library.

Authors: Heidi Foxford, Aidan Gill, Dorothy Warren
Commissioning editor: Joanna Ramsay
Development editors and copyeditors: Anna Clark, Fiona McDonald, Tony Wayte
Proofreader: David Hemsley
Cover designer: The Big Mountain Design
Production controller: Katharine Willard

p79 l= Breck P. Kent/Shutterstock r= Breck P. Kent/Shutterstock, p80 l=Tina Gutierrez/Shutterstock r=Sang Low PS/Shutterstock.

The publishers gratefully acknowledge the permission granted to reproduce the copyright material in this book. Every effort has been made to trace copyright holders and to obtain their permission for the use of copyright material. The publishers will gladly receive any information enabling them to rectify any error or omission at the first opportunity.

Contents

Part 2 Tests

Mark Schemes

Introduction

Collins KS3 Science Progress Tests provide an independent way of regularly assessing pupils' progress every half term and at the start of Year 7 and Year 8. They are also suitable for Third Level Science in Scotland.

Baseline Tests

There are two baseline tests: one for Year 7 and one for Year 8. The initial baseline tests help you to find out what your students know and don't know from Key Stage 2 and Year 7 respectively and to decide if they should take the 'core' or 'extended' tests. Each baseline test is worth 60 marks.

Half termly tests

The tests are designed to be used at the end of each half term for Year 7 and Year 8.

Each half termly test has a 'core' and 'extended' option. These are two different levels and you can choose the level you think will best suit your student, using their baseline test performance to help you. The 'extended' tests are for students working at greater depth and challenge.

A student can move between 'core' and 'extended' tests as you see fit. There are occasionally some common questions between the 'core' and 'extended' tests for a topic.

Questions within each test are ramped by demand. The tests include questions with a range of different marks, testing knowledge and understanding (AO1), application of knowledge and understanding (AO2) and analysis (AO3) at KS3 demand. The questions use GCSE 9-1 command words.

Maths skills and practical skills questions are embedded throughout.

How to use this book
There are six tests for each science in Part 1 and six tests for each science in Part 2, designed to be used at the end of each half term of Year 7 and Year 8. Each test is available at both 'core' and 'extended' level and is worth 16 marks.

You can set the tests individually as 16-mark tests or you can combine one Physics, one Chemistry and one Biology test to give a 48-mark test.

The tests can be used flexibly across Years 7, 8 and 9 to suit your teaching. Part 2 tests are at a higher level of demand than the Part 1 tests and may assume knowledge from Part 1 so we would recommend setting Part 1 tests before Part 2 tests.

The questions test knowledge from the 2014 National Curriculum Programme of Study for Key Stage 3 Science and also cover the AQA KS3 syllabus (please see the Curriculum Matching Charts) but you can use the tests to follow your scheme of work. The tests are editable for further flexibility.

Marking the tests
An easy-to-use mark scheme and answers are provided to show you how the marks are allocated. We have also offered some guidance on indicative target GCSE 9-1 grade performance based on a judgement of the level of demand of each test. Please bear in mind that progress is not always linear and that teachers remain the best judge of student performance.

Recording progress
You can use the student record sheet to provide evidence of which areas your students have performed well in and where they need to focus, including different AO-style questions, maths skills and practical skills. Two spreadsheets are provided in the downloadable version. The summary spreadsheet allow you to easily record results for your classes, and identify any gaps in understanding. The detailed spreadsheet tracker allows you to enter results for each question and perform question-level analysis for more in-depth planning of your next teaching and learning steps.

Editable download
All the files are available in Word format for you to edit if you wish. Go to Collins.co.uk/assessment/downloads to find the instructions on how to download. The files are password protected and the password clue is included on the website. You will need to use the clue to locate the password in your book.

Curriculum Matching Chart

Biology Tests

Test (core and extended)	AQA KS3 Syllabus Reference	2014 Key Stage 3 Science Programme of Study reference
Part 1		
Organisms: Skeletal and muscular systems	3.8.1 Organisms: Movement	The structure and functions of the human skeleton, to include support, protection, movement and making blood cells Biomechanics – the interaction between skeleton and muscles, including the measurement of force exerted by different muscles The function of muscles and examples of antagonistic muscles
Organisms: Cells to systems	3.8.2 Organisms: Cells	The hierarchical organisation of multicellular organisms: from cells to tissues to organs to systems to organisms Cells as the fundamental unit of living organisms, including how to observe, interpret and record cell structure using a light microscope The functions of the cell wall, cell membrane, cytoplasm, nucleus, vacuole, mitochondria and chloroplasts The similarities and differences between animal and plant cells The role of diffusion in the movement of materials in and between cells
Ecosystems and habitats	3.9.1 Ecosystems: Interdependence	The interdependence of organisms in an ecosystem, including food webs and insect pollinated crops How organisms affect, and are affected by, their environment, including the accumulation of toxic materials The importance of plant reproduction through insect pollination in human food security
Plant reproduction	3.9.2 Ecosystems: Plant reproduction	Reproduction in plants, including flower structure, wind and insect pollination, fertilisation Reproduction in plants, including seed and fruit formation and dispersal, including quantitative investigation of some dispersal mechanisms
Variation	3.10.1 Genes: Variation	The variation between individuals within a species being continuous or discontinuous, to include measurement and graphical representation of variation Differences between species
Human reproduction	3.10.2 Genes: Human reproduction	Reproduction in humans (as an example of a mammal), including the structure and function of the male and female reproductive systems, menstrual cycle (without details of hormones), gametes, fertilisation, gestation and birth to include the effect of maternal lifestyle on the foetus through the placenta

Test (core and extended)	AQA KS3 Syllabus Reference	2014 Key Stage 3 Science Programme of Study reference
Part 2		
Human reproduction	3.10.2 Genes: Human reproduction	Reproduction in humans (as an example of a mammal), including the structure and function of the male and female reproductive systems, menstrual cycle (without details of hormones), gametes, fertilisation, gestation and birth to include the effect of maternal lifestyle on the foetus through the placenta
Breathing and gas exchange	3.8.3 Organisms: Breathing	The mechanism of breathing to move air in and out of the lungs, using a pressure model to explain the movement of gases including simple measurements of lung volume
The structure and functions of the gas exchange system in humans, including adaptations to function
The impact of exercise, asthma and smoking on the human gas exchange system
The role of leaf stomata in gas exchange in plants
Digestion	3.8.4 Organisms: Digestion	The importance of bacteria in the human digestive system
The content of a healthy human diet: carbohydrates, lipids (fats and oils), proteins, vitamins, minerals, dietary fibre and water, and why each is needed
Calculations of energy requirements in a healthy daily diet
The consequences of imbalances in the diet including obesity, starvation and deficiency diseases
The tissues and organs of the human digestive system, including adaptations to function
Respiration	3.9.3 Ecosystems: Respiration	Aerobic and anaerobic respiration in living organisms, including the breakdown of organic molecules to enable all the other chemical processes necessary for life
A word summary for aerobic respiration
The process of anaerobic respiration in humans and micro-organisms, including fermentation, and a word summary for anaerobic respiration
The differences between aerobic and anaerobic respiration in terms of the reactants, the products formed and the implications for the organism
Photosynthesis	3.9.4 Ecosystems: Photosynthesis	The reactants in, and products of, photosynthesis, and a word summary for photosynthesis
The dependence of almost all life on Earth on the ability of photosynthetic organisms, such as plants and algae, to use sunlight in photosynthesis to build organic molecules that are an essential energy store and to maintain levels of oxygen and carbon dioxide in the atmosphere
The adaptations of leaves for photosynthesis
Evolution, extinction and biodiversity	3.10.3 Genes: Evolution	The variation between species and between individuals of the same species meaning some organisms compete more successfully, which can drive natural selection
Changes in the environment which may leave individuals within a species, and some entire species, less well adapted to compete successfully and reproduce, which in turn may lead to extinction
The importance of maintaining biodiversity and the use of gene banks to preserve hereditary material
Genes and inheritance	3.10.4 Genes: Inheritance	A simple model of chromosomes, genes and DNA in heredity, including the part played by Watson, Crick, Wilkins and Franklin in the development of the DNA model
Heredity as the process by which genetic information is transmitted from one generation to the next

Chemistry Tests

Test (core and extended)	AQA KS3 Syllabus Reference	2014 Key Stage 3 Science Programme of Study reference
Part 1		
The particulate nature of matter	3.5.1 Matter: Particle model	The properties of the different states of matter (solid, liquid and gas) in terms of the particle model, including gas pressure Diffusion in liquids and gases driven by differences in concentration Diffusion in terms of the particle model Changes of state in terms of the particle model The differences in arrangements, in motion and in closeness of particles explaining changes of state, shape and density; the anomaly of ice–water transition Atoms and molecules as particles
Pure and impure substances	3.5.2 Matter. Separating mixtures	The concept of a pure substance Mixtures, including dissolving Simple techniques for separating mixtures: filtration, evaporation, distillation and chromatography The identification of pure substances
Acids and alkalis	3.6.2 Reactions: Acids and alkalis	Defining acids and alkalis in terms of neutralisation reactions The pH scale for measuring acidity/alkalinity; and indicators Reactions of acids with alkalis to produce a salt plus water
Chemical reactions of metals and non-metals	3.6.1 Reactions: metals and non-metals	The varying physical and chemical properties of different elements The properties of metals and non-metals Reactions of acids with metals to produce a salt plus hydrogen The order of metals and carbon in the reactivity series Representing chemical reactions using formulas and using equations Displacement reactions Changes of state and chemical reactions Combustion, thermal decomposition, oxidation and displacement reactions
Earth and rocks	3.7.1 Earth: Earth structure	The composition of the Earth The structure of the Earth The rock cycle and the formation of igneous, sedimentary and metamorphic rocks
Dalton's atomic theory		A simple (Dalton) atomic model Differences between atoms, elements and compounds Chemical symbols and formulae for elements and compounds Conservation of mass changes of state and chemical reactions

Test (core and extended)	AQA KS3 Syllabus Reference	2014 Key Stage 3 Science Programme of Study reference
Part 2		
The periodic table	3.5.3 Matter: Periodic table	The principles underpinning the Mendeleev periodic table The periodic table: periods and groups; metals and non-metals The varying physical and chemical properties of different elements How patterns in reactions can be predicted with reference to the periodic table The properties of metals and non-metals
Materials	3.5.4 Matter: Elements	The chemical properties of metal and non-metal oxides with respect to acidity Properties of ceramics, polymers and composites (qualitative) Differences between atoms, elements and compounds
Energetics	3.6.3 Reactions: Chemical energy	Internal energy stored in materials Energy changes on changes of state (qualitative) Exothermic and endothermic chemical reactions (qualitative); What catalysts do
Chemical reactions	3.6.4 Reactions: Types of reaction	Chemical reactions as the rearrangement of atoms Representing chemical reactions using formulae and using equations Exothermic and endothermic chemical reactions (qualitative); Combustion, thermal decomposition, oxidation and displacement reactions Chemical symbols and formulae for elements and compounds Conservation of mass changes of state and chemical reactions
The atmosphere	3.7.3 Earth: Climate	The composition of the atmosphere The production of carbon dioxide by human activity and the impact on climate.
The Earth's resources	3.7.4 Earth: Earth resources	Earth as a source of limited resources and the efficacy of recycling The order of metals and carbon in the reactivity series The use of carbon in obtaining metals from metal oxides

Physics Tests

Test (core and extended)	AQA KS3 Syllabus Reference	2014 Key Stage 3 Science Programme of Study reference
Part 1		
Movement: speed and acceleration	3.1.1 Forces: Speed	Speed and the quantitative relationship between average speed, distance and time (speed = distance ÷ time) The representation of a journey on a distance–time graph Forces being needed to cause objects to stop or start moving, or to change their speed or direction of motion (qualitative only) Change depending on direction of force and its size Describing motion: relative motion: trains and cars passing one another
Forces and gravity	3.1.2 Forces: Gravity	Gravity force, weight = mass × gravitational field strength (g), on Earth g = 10 N/kg, different on other planets and stars Force measured in newtons Gravity forces between Earth and Moon, and between Earth and Sun (qualitative only)
Electric circuits: current, potential difference and resistance	3.2.1 Electromagnets: Voltage and resistance	Electric current, measured in amperes, in circuits, series and parallel circuits, currents add where branches meet and current as flow of charge Potential difference, measured in volts, battery and bulb ratings Resistance, measured in ohms, as the ratio of potential difference (p.d.) to current Differences in resistance between conducting and insulating components (quantitative)
Static electricity	3.2.2 Electromagnets: Current	Non-contact forces: forces due to static electricity. Separation of positive or negative charges when objects are rubbed together: transfer of electrons, forces between charged objects The idea of electric field, forces acting across the space between objects not in contact
Energy: stores, transfers, power and costs	3.3.1 Energy: Energy costs and 3.3.2 Energy: Energy transfer	Comparing energy values of different foods (from labels) (kJ) Comparing power ratings of appliances in watts (W, kW) Comparing amounts of energy transferred (J, kJ, kW hour) Domestic fuel bills, fuel use and costs Fuels and energy resources Energy as a quantity that can be quantified and calculated; the total energy has the same value before and after a change Other processes that involve energy transfer: changing motion, dropping an object, completing an electrical circuit, stretching a spring, metabolism of food, burning fuels Using physical processes and mechanisms, rather than energy, to explain the intermediate steps that bring about such changes Comparing the starting with the final conditions of a system and describing increases and decreases in the amounts of energy associated with movements, changes in positions in a field, in elastic distortions and in chemical compositions Work done and energy changes on deformation
The Earth in space	3.7.2 Earth: Universe	Our Sun as a star, other stars in our galaxy, other galaxies The seasons and the Earth's tilt, day length at different times of year, in different hemispheres The light year as a unit of astronomical distance Understand that scientific methods and theories develop as earlier explanations are modified to take account of new evidence and ideas

Test (core and extended)	AQA KS3 Syllabus Reference	2014 Key Stage 3 Science Programme of Study reference
Part 2		
Sound	3.4.1 Waves: Sound	Sound needs a medium to travel, the speed of sound in air, in water, in solids Frequencies of sound waves, measured in hertz (Hz); echoes, reflection and absorption of sound Pressure waves transferring energy; use for cleaning and physiotherapy by ultrasound Sound produced by vibrations of objects, in loud speakers, detected by their effects on microphone diaphragm and the ear drum; sound waves are longitudinal The auditory range of humans and animals
Contact forces, moments and pressure	3.1.3 Forces: Contact forces and 3.1.4 Forces: Pressure	Forces as pushes or pulls, arising from the interaction between two objects Using force arrows in diagrams, adding forces in1 dimension, balanced and unbalanced forces Moment as the turning effect of a force Forces: associated with deforming objects; stretching and squashing – springs; with rubbing and friction between surfaces, with pushing things out of the way; resistance to motion of air and water Forces measured in newtons, measurements of stretch or compression as force is changed Forces–extension linear relation; Hooke's Law as a special case Atmospheric pressure, decreases with increase of height as weight of air above decreases with height Pressure in liquids, increasing with depth; upthrust effects, floating and sinking Pressure measured by ratio of force over area – acting normal to any surface Opposing forces and equilibrium: weight held by stretched spring or supported on a compressed surface
Light	3.4.2 Waves: Light	Light waves travelling through a vacuum; speed of light The transmission of light through materials: absorption, diffuse scattering and specular reflection at a surface Use of ray model to explain imaging in mirrors, the pinhole camera, the refraction of light and action of convex lens in focusing (qualitative); the human eye Light transferring energy from source to absorber leading to chemical and electrical effects; photosensitive material in the retina and in cameras Colours and the different frequencies of light, white light and prisms (qualitative only); differential colour effects in absorption and diffuse reflection
Magnetism and electromagnetism	3.2.3 Electromagnets: Electromagnets 3.2.4 Electromagnets: Magnetism	Non-contact forces: forces between magnets Magnetic poles, attraction and repulsion Magnetic fields by plotting with compass, representation by field lines Earth's magnetism, compass and navigation The magnetic effect of a current, electromagnets, DC motors (principles only).

Energy: work done, heating and cooling	3.3.3 Energy: Work and 3.3.4 Energy: Heating and cooling	Simple machines give bigger force but at the expense of smaller movement (and vice versa): product of force and displacement unchanged Heating and thermal equilibrium: temperature difference between 2 objects leading to energy transfer from the hotter to the cooler one, through contact (conduction) or radiation; such transfers tending to reduce the temperature difference: use of insulators Changes with temperature in motion and spacing of particles Comparing the starting with the final conditions of a system and describing the amount of energy associated with increases and decreases in temperature
Waves: properties and effects	3.4.3 Waves: Wave effects and 3.4.4 Waves: Wave properties	The similarities and differences between light waves and waves in matter Light waves travelling through a vacuum; speed of light Sound needs a medium to travel, the speed of sound in air, in water, in solids Waves on water as undulations which travel through water with transverse motion; these waves can be reflected, and add or cancel – superposition Waves transferring information for conversion to electrical signals by microphone

Year 7 Baseline Test: Biology

1 A student finds some organisms in the school grounds.

The diagram shows the organisms the student finds.

stick insect   jumping spider   meal moth   blackbird

not to scale

a. Name **two** organisms shown in the diagram that have wings. **[1 mark]**

1 _____

2 _____

b. The jumping spider can eat the meal moth.

What is the name for an animal that is eaten by something else?

Tick **one** box. **[1 mark]**

Predator ☐

Prey ☐

Producer ☐

Primate ☐

c. A student makes a classification key to identify the organisms in the diagram.

Using the information in the classification key, write the name of each organism in the correct box on the key. One has been done for you. **[2 marks]**

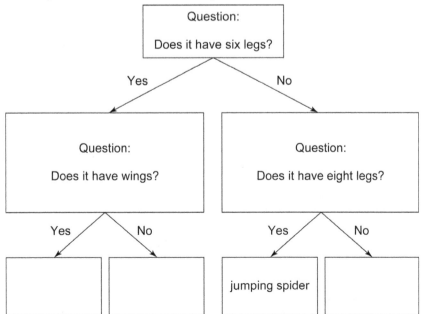

d. A blackbird is a vertebrate.

What is a vertebrate?

Tick **one** box.   [1 mark]

An organism that has wings ☐

An organism that has a beak ☐

An organism that has a backbone ☐

An organism with legs ☐

2 A student is investigating leaf length in different trees. Her results are shown in the table.

Tree	Average leaf length (cm)
A	5.5
B	7.0
C	4.5

a. Complete the bar chart to show the average leaf length of the different trees.

The first one has been done for you.   [2 marks]

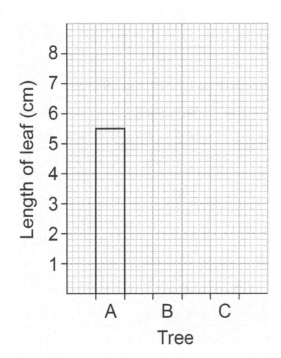

b. Name a piece of equipment that the student would need to use to measure the length of the leaves.   [1 mark]

_____

c. Trees are living organisms.

Tick the boxes to show what trees can do.

Tick **two** boxes.   [2 marks]

They can reproduce. ☐

They can breathe. ☐

They can eat food. ☐

They can grow. ☐

d. For healthy growth a tree needs air, light and nutrients from the soil.

Name **one** other thing plants need to live.

_____   [1 mark]

3 An owl has sharp hooked claws called talons.

Suggest how talons could help an owl survive.   [2 marks]

_____

_____

4 Draw **one** line from each part of the body to its function.   [3 marks]

Part of body	Function
heart	tubes that carry blood around the body
blood vessels	an organ that pumps blood around the body
blood	an organ that is involved in digestion
stomach	a liquid that transports nutrients around the body

5 A man decides to start exercising every day.

What long-term effect is exercise likely to have on his heart?

Tick **one** box. [1 mark]

The man's heart will get stronger. ☐

The man's heart will get blocked. ☐

The man's heart will get too warm. ☐

The man's heart will not change. ☐

6 A scientist measures a man's heart rate while he runs for 4 minutes. The table shows the results.

Time (minutes)	Heart rate (beats per minute)
0	67
1	89
2	98
3	102
4	104

a. What was the man's heart rate at 3 minutes into the exercise? [1 mark]

_____bpm

b. What variable was the scientist measuring? [1 mark]

_____

c. What can the scientist conclude from the results?

Tick **one** box. [1 mark]

A heart can only beat for 4 minutes. ☐

Exercise increases the heart rate. ☐

Exercise decreases the heart rate. ☐

Exercise does not affect the heart rate. ☐

Total marks _____ /20

Year 7 Baseline Test: Chemistry

1   A student was playing in the garden when he noticed a bucket filled with nails, small stones and sand. He decided to separate the mixture.

The diagram shows some equipment than can be used to separate mixtures.

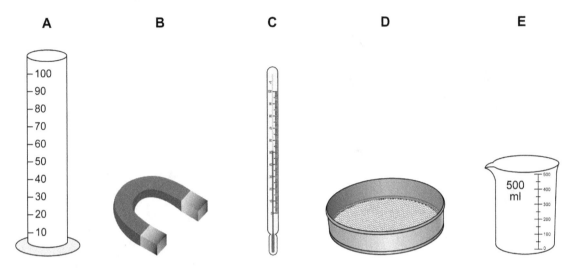

A   B   C   D   E

a.   Identify the equipment that the student could use to separate nails.

Write **one** letter.   [1 mark]

_____

b.   Give a reason for your answer.   [2 marks]

_____

_____

c.   Next, he wanted to separate the small stones from the sand.

Identify the piece of equipment he should use.

Write **one** letter.   [1 mark]

_____

d.   Give a reason for your answer.   [2 marks]

_____

_____

2 The diagram shows the water cycle.

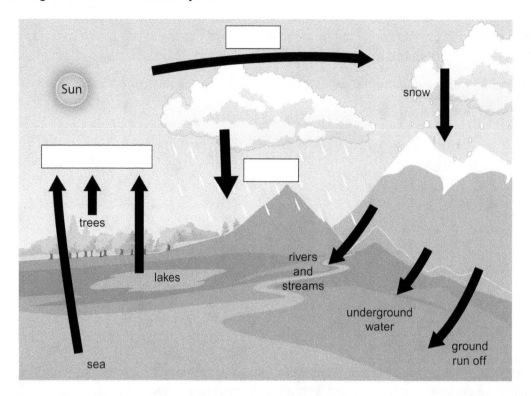

Complete the diagram. **[3 marks]**

3 A student is investigating dissolving.

She measures out 20 cm³ of water and pours it into a beaker. She then adds 1 g of salt and stirs the mixture. She repeats the process until no more salt will dissolve.

The diagram shows some equipment used to make measurements.

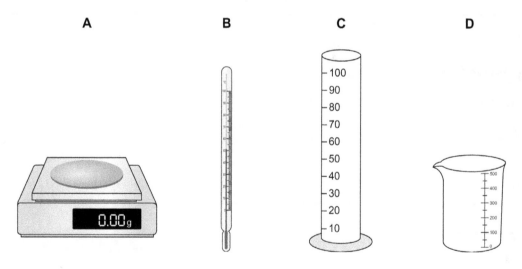

a. Identify the piece of equipment the student used to measure the volume of water.

Write **one** letter. **[1 mark]**

_____

b. Identify the piece of equipment the student used to measure the mass of salt.

Write **one** letter. **[1 mark]**

_____

c. Describe the change that took place when the mixture was stirred. [2 marks]

_____

_____

d. Describe how the student could take the temperature of the mixture. [2 marks]

_____

_____

4 A class is investigating how different materials change.

Two students have different ideas about what happens when a candle burns.

When a candle burns a non-reversible change takes place.

When a candle burns the wax just melts.

Student A   Student B

The students light a candle and make some observations.

They record their observations in a table.

Observation	Evidence of a reversible or non-reversible change?
smoke is given off	non reversible
the wax at the top changes from solid to liquid	_____
the candle gets shorter	_____

a. Complete the table. The first row has been completed for you. [1 mark]

b. Identify which student statement is correct. Give a reason for your answer. [2 marks]

_____

_____

Next the following experiment is set up.

20 cm³ of vinegar is put in a plastic bottle.

5 g of bicarbonate of soda is put in a balloon.

A balloon is then put on top of the bottle as shown in the diagram.

The balloon is held up so that the bicarbonate of soda falls into the bottle.

At the start   After 10 minutes

c. Describe what happened to the balloon during the experiment.

Suggest a reason for your answer.   [2 marks]

_____

_____

Total marks _____ /20

Year 7 Baseline Test: Physics

1 Complete the following sentences. Use words from the list.   **[4 marks]**

> **fall   weight   gravity   mass**

On Earth, objects that are dropped _____ to the ground.

The amount of substance in an object is called its _____.

There is a force on each object called its _____.

This force is produced by _____.

2 The diagram shows a skydiver with an open parachute. Each arrow shows a force acting on the skydiver and parachute.

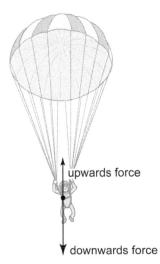

upwards force

downwards force

a. Give the name of the force that acts downwards. _____ **[1 mark]**

b. Give the name of the force that acts upwards. _____ **[1 mark]**

3 The diagram shows a model of the Earth and the Moon.

Earth (person)   Moon   bright lamp

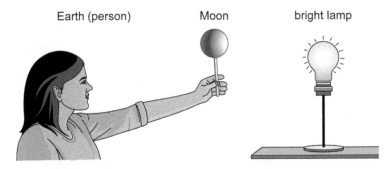

a. What is the name of the object from the Solar System represented by the bright lamp model?

_____ **[1 mark]**

b. The Moon does not make its own light. Describe how we can see the Moon.   **[1 mark]**

_____

_____

4   The diagram shows an experiment to show how shadows are formed.

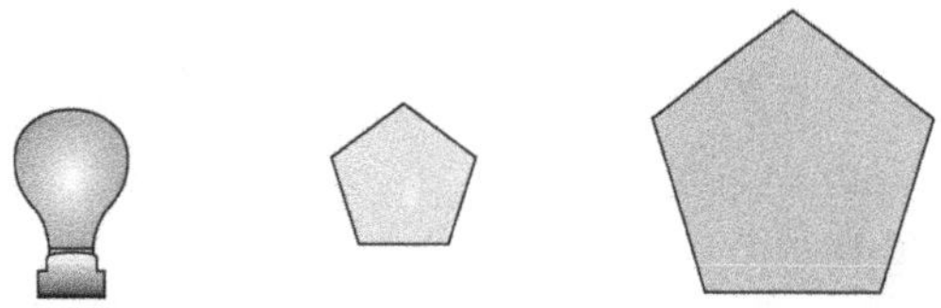

lamp   shape   shadow

The shape of the shadow formed is the same shape as the object.

What does this evidence tell us about light?

Tick one box.   [1 mark]

The evidence (the shape of the shadow) tells us that …

light is made up of many colours.   ☐

light bends around corners.   ☐

light travels in straight lines.   ☐

the object is transparent (it lets all light through it).   ☐

5   The diagram shows an electric circuit for Experiment 1.

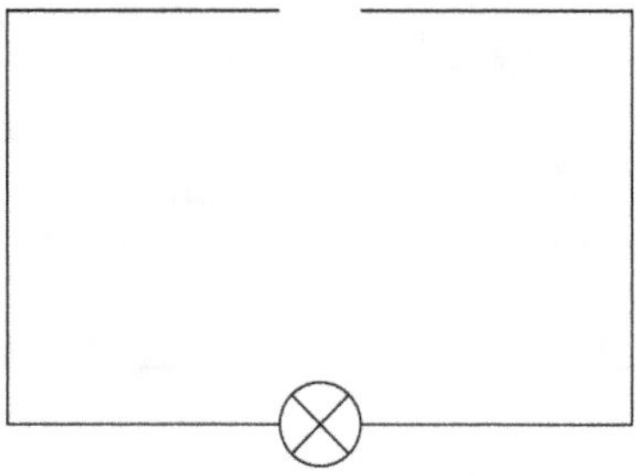

a.   The circuit is not complete. Give the name of the component needed to complete the circuit.

_____   [1 mark]

b.   Draw the circuit symbol for this component on the diagram.   [1 mark]

c.   For Experiment 2, a student adds another lamp to the circuit connected end-to-end
     with the first lamp.

     What will happen to the brightness of the lamps, compared to the lamp in Experiment 1?

     Tick **one** box.   [1 mark]

     Both lamps will shine more brightly than Experiment 1.   ☐

     Both lamps will shine with the same brightness as Experiment 1.   ☐

     Both lamps will shine less brightly than Experiment 1.   ☐

6 The wires used to connect components in electric circuits are usually made of copper.

For each statement about copper, choose whether it is **True** or **False**.

Tick **one** box for **each** statement. [3 marks]

Statement	True	False
Copper is a good conductor	☐	☐
Copper is easily shaped	☐	☐
Copper melts at a low temperature	☐	☐

7 A student sets up an experiment to investigate different lengths of lever.

The table shows the results.

Measurement	Length of lever (cm)	Weight of object being lifted (N)	Force needed to balance the weight (N)
A	40	20	20
B	60	20	10
C	80	20	9
D	100	20	5
E	120	20	4

a. Name the independent variable (the variable the student changed before each measurement).

[1 mark]

_____

b. Describe the pattern in the measurements. [1 mark]

As the lever gets _____, the force needed to move the weight gets _____.

The diagram shows the force–length graph the student started to draw to show her results.

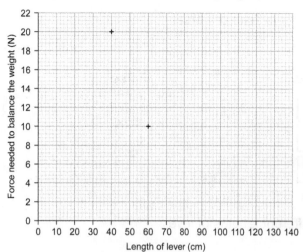

Force needed to balance the weight (N) — vertical axis (0 to 22)

Length of lever (cm) — horizontal axis (0 to 140)

c. Complete plotting the points on the graph.   [2 marks]

d. The graph should be a smooth curve. Identify the measurement that appears to be wrong.

Tick **one** box.   [1 mark]

☐   ☐   ☐   ☐   ☐

A   B   C   D   E

Total marks _____ /20

Year 8 Baseline Test: Biology

1 The diagram shows a food chain.

Grass ⟶ Grasshopper ⟶ Mouse ⟶ Owl

  a. A producer is an organism that makes its own food using energy from the Sun.

   Name the **producer** in the food chain.   **[1 mark]**

   _____

  b. Name the **primary consumer** in the food chain.   **[1 mark]**

   _____

  c. What do the arrows in a food chain represent?   **[1 mark]**

   _____

  d. The number of mice in the food chain suddenly **decreases**.

   Predict how this may affect the number of glass plants.   **[2 marks]**

   _____

   _____

2 The diagram shows a synovial joint.

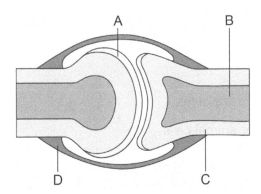

  a. Cartilage is a tough, smooth tissue that covers the ends of bones.

   Which letter shows cartilage?   **[1 mark]**

   _____

b. What is produced in **B**? [1 mark]

_____

c. The part labelled **D** shows a ligament.

Describe the function a ligament. [1 mark]

_____

3 Draw **one** line to match each part of the male reproductive system to its function. [2 marks]

Part of male reproductive system	Function
testes	the tube that carries sperm from the testes to the urethra during ejaculation
sperm duct	the tube that carries urine or sperm to the tip of the penis
urethra	where sperm are made

4 Which of the following is an example of an **organ**?

Tick **one** box. [1 mark]

Hair ☐

The stomach ☐

The nervous system ☐

A nucleus ☐

5 A science technician has found two slides, **A** and **B**, in a classroom.

The technician needs to know if the slides contain plant or animal cells.

	Cells on slide A	Cells on slide B
nucleus	✓	✓
cell membrane	✓	✓
cell wall	✓	✗
chloroplasts	✓	✗

a. Which slide shows a **plant cell**?

Tick **one** box. [1 mark]

Slide **A** ☐

Slide **B** ☐

Slides **A** and **B** ☐

It is impossible to tell ☐

b. Explain your answer. [2 marks]

_____

_____

6 The table shows some different types of seeds.

Complete the table to show which type of dispersal is most likely for each seed.

Give the features of the seed that allow it to be dispersed in that way.

The first one has been done for you. [2 marks]

Type of seed		Type of seed dispersal	Features of seed that allow it to be dispersed
tomato 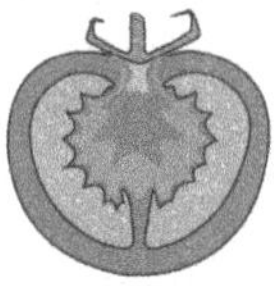	tomato	animal	it is a brightly coloured and tasty fruit that contains seeds with indigestible coats
sandbur 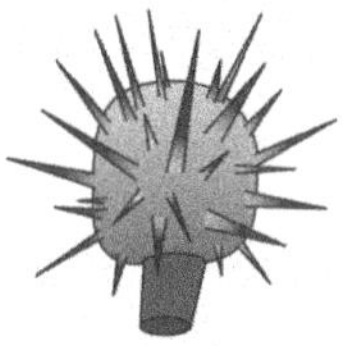	sandbur		
dandelion 	dandelion		

7   Which of the following best describes a **gene**?

Tick **one** box.   [1 mark]

A cell that carries genetic information

A damaged section of DNA

A section of DNA that has instructions for a characteristic

A part of sperm and egg cells

8   The graph shows the variation in the heights of a population of people.

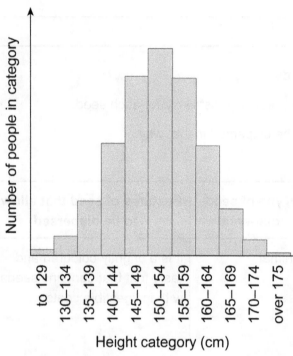

a.   The shape of the graph is called a **normal distribution**.

Why is the graph this shape?   [1 mark]

_____

b.   Name the type of variation shown in the chart.

Explain your answer.   [2 marks]

Type of variation: _____

Explanation: _____

_____

Total marks _____ /20

Year 8 Baseline Test: Chemistry

1 **a.** Three pairs of chemicals are listed below.

Draw **one** line from each reaction to the correct result when they are mixed together.   **[2 marks]**

Pair of chemicals	Result
calcium + hydrochloric acid	calcium chloride and water are formed
calcium carbonate + hydrochloric acid	calcium chloride and hydrogen gas are formed
calcium hydroxide + hydrochloric acid	calcium chloride, water and carbon dioxide are formed

A group of students used a pH sensor to investigate how the pH changed during a chemical reaction.

They measured out 10 cm^3 of hydrochloric acid and poured it into a small beaker and recorded the pH before adding some calcium hydroxide.

b. Predict the pH at the start of the reaction.   **[1 mark]**

_____

c. Name the type of reaction the students were investigating.   **[1 mark]**

_____

d. Describe how the pH will change during the reaction.   **[2 marks]**

_____

_____

_____

2 A student was investigating the density of some materials.

He weighed a 1 cm³ cube of each material.

He recorded the results in a table.

Material	Metal or non-metal?	Mass (g)
wood	non-metal	2.2
plastic	_____	1.0
aluminium	_____	10.2
lead	metal	21.4

a. Complete the table.   [1 mark]

b. Identify the dependent variable.   [1 mark]

_____

c. Write down a variable that must be controlled.   [1 mark]

_____

d. State **one** conclusion you can draw from these results.   [1 mark]

_____

_____

e. Suggest a reason why the mass of lead is greater than the mass of aluminium.   [2 marks]

_____

_____

_____

3 Part of the reactivity series of metals is shown below.

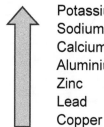

Increasing reactivity

Potassium
Sodium
Calcium
Aluminium
Zinc
Lead
Copper

a. Use the information given in the reactivity series.

Identify **one** metal that would react with aluminium nitrate in a displacement reaction.

Circle **one** term.   [1 mark]

    zinc   **potassium**   **lead**   **aluminium**

When a piece of calcium was placed in a solution of copper sulfate the following observations were made.

- The solution went from blue to colourless.
- The piece of calcium got smaller.
- An orange–pink solid started to form.

b.   Explain these observations.   [3 marks]

_____

_____

_____

_____

4   The diagram shows the equipment used to carry out the simple distillation of seawater.

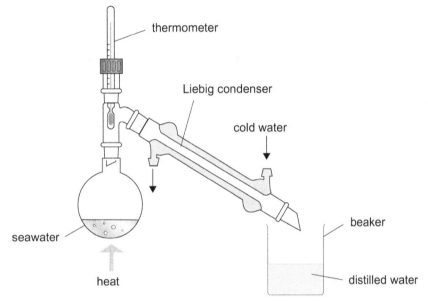

a.   Use your ideas about particle theory to explain how the sample of distilled water
     is obtained.   [3 marks]

_____

_____

_____

_____

_____

b.   Describe how you could obtain a sample of salt crystals from the seawater.   [1 mark]

_____

_____

Total marks _____ /20

Year 8 Baseline Test: Physics

1 Name the device used to measure potential difference in an electric circuit.   **[1 mark]**

_____

2 Draw **one** line from each energy store to the correct description.   **[3 marks]**

Word	Definition

| kinetic energy store | changes when an object is warmed up |

| gravitational potential energy store | changes when an object is stretched or compressed |

| thermal energy store | changes when an object is raised up |

| elastic energy store | changes when an object speeds up |

3 The circuit diagram shows an electric circuit with a battery, four ammeters and two resistors. The current measured by each ammeter is shown in the table.

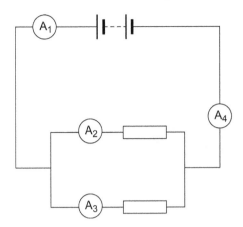

Use your knowledge of series and parallel circuits to complete the table.   **[2 marks]**

Ammeter number	Ammeter reading, current (A)
1	0.8
2	0.4
3	_____
4	_____

4 After a person combs their hair with a plastic comb, they hold the comb so it almost touches the hair. Their hair lifts up in the direction of the comb.

Explain what has happened.   **[3 marks]**

_____

_____

_____

5 The experimental diagram shows a toy car set up on a sloping track. The car is held still at the top of the ramp.

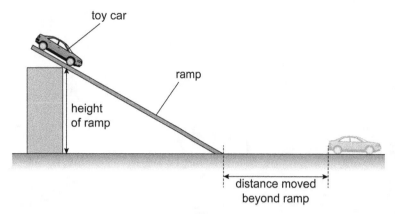

a. The car is held above the ground. Give the name of the main energy store at this time.   **[1 mark]**

_____

b. The car is released and it rolls down the ramp. Describe the energy transfer that takes place.

[1 mark]

_____

The diagram shows the distance–time graph for the movement of the car as it rolls down the ramp.

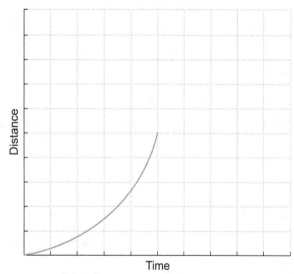

c. Choose the correct description for the car's movement as it rolls down the ramp.   **[1 mark]**

Tick **one** box.

The car is:

Stationary   ☐

Moving at a constant speed   ☐

Moving and accelerating   ☐

Moving and decelerating   ☐

When it reaches the end of the ramp, the car moves onto a rough, flat surface.

d. Choose the correct description for the car's movement on the flat surface, in the moments after it has left the ramp. **[1 mark]**

Stationary ☐

Moving at a constant speed ☐

Moving and accelerating ☐

Moving and decelerating ☐

e. Draw a line on the distance–time graph to show this movement. (Sketch the graph. It does not need to be accurately plotted.) **[3 marks]**

6 The table shows part of an electricity bill.

Meter readings				
Period	**Meter number**	**Start reading/kW h**	**End reading/kW h**	**Reader** E = estimate C = customer A = actual
1 Jan to 30 Mar	S088 54321	07464	09201	C
1 Apr to 30 Jun	S088 54321	09201	11018	E
Energy used from 1 Jan to 30 Jun	2554 kW h			
Price per kW h	5.5 p		Total bill	£140.47

a. There is an error in this bill. Identify and describe the error. **[1 mark]**

_____

_____

b. Calculate the correct total bill, in pounds and pence. You **must** show your working. **[3 marks]**

_____

_____

_____

_____

Total marks _____ /20

Biology – Organisms: skeletal and muscular systems

1 The human skeleton supports the body and gives it its shape.

Which of the following are other functions of the skeleton?

Tick **two** boxes. [2 marks]

To allow movement ☐

To make hormones ☐

To protect organs ☐

To insulate the body ☐

2 The skull, which surrounds the brain, is made from bones.

What is the most important function of the skull? [1 mark]

_____

3 Name the part of the body where red blood cells are made.

Circle **one** term. [1 mark]

muscles   **ligaments**   **cartilage**   **bone marrow**

4 The diagram shows the elbow joint in the arm.

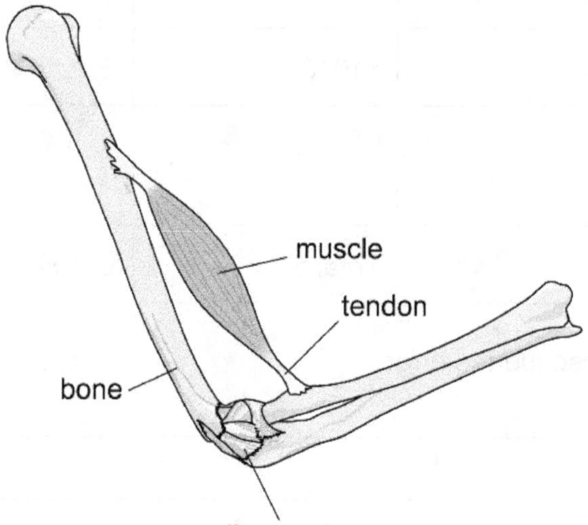

a. The muscle shown in the diagram contracts.

Describe what will happen to the arm. [1 mark]

_____

b. A ligament attaches one bone to another bone.

What do tendons attach to bone? [1 mark]

_____

5 An athlete has injured a large muscle in his leg.

Explain why an injured muscle could make it difficult for the athlete to run. **[2 marks]**

_____

_____

6 Different types of joint are found in the body.

Draw **one** line to connect each type of joint to the movement allowed by that joint. **[2 marks]**

Type of joint	Movement allowed

hinge	forwards, backwards and rotation

ball and socket	forwards and backwards

pivot	rotation around an axis

7 Name an example of a ball and socket joint that is found in the body. **[1 mark]**

_____

8 The diagram shows the quadriceps and hamstring muscles in a leg. They are antagonistic muscles.

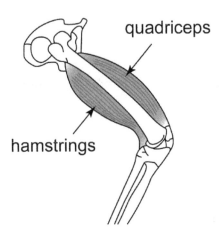

quadriceps

hamstrings

Complete the table by writing **contracts** or **relaxes** to show the action of the quadriceps and hamstring muscles in each type of movement. **[2 marks]**

Muscle	Bending the leg	Straightening the leg
quadriceps		
hamstring		

9 A handgrip dynamometer is an instrument that is used to test the strength of muscles in the forearm and hand. A rock climber uses the handgrip dynamometer to measure the force exerted by the muscles in her hand and forearm muscles.

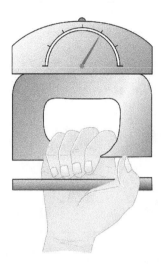

She takes one measurement at the end of each week, for 6 weeks.

Week	1	2	3	4	5	6
Force (N)	56.3	57.1	58.0	58.7	47.2	47.0

a. What was the strength of the climber's grip in week 2?

_____ N   **[1 mark]**

b. In which week did the climber have the strongest grip?

Week _____   **[1 mark]**

c. Which statement best describes how the climber's forearm and hand strength changed over the 6 weeks.

Tick **one** box.   **[1 mark]**

It increased   ☐

It decreased   ☐

It stayed the same   ☐

It increased then decreased   ☐

Total marks _____ /16

Biology – Organisms: skeletal and muscular systems

1 The human skeleton supports the body and gives it its shape.

Describe **two** other functions of the skeleton. [2 marks]

1 _____

2 _____

2 The cranium is part of the human skull that surrounds the brain.

What is the most important function of the cranium? [1 mark]

_____

3 In what part of the body are red blood cells made?

Circle **one** term. [1 mark]

   muscles   **ligaments**   **cartilage**   **bone marrow**

4 Different types of joints are found in the body.

Complete the table to show the differences between a hinge joint and a ball and socket joint.

[2 marks]

Type of joint	Movement allowed	Example in body
hinge		elbow, knee
ball and socket	backwards and forwards and all directions, rotation	

5 The diagram shows the elbow joint found in the arm.

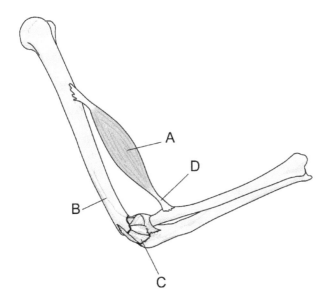

a. State the letter on the diagram that shows a ligament. [1 mark]

_____

b. State the letter on the diagram that shows a tendon. [1 mark]

_____

6 An athlete has injured a tendon in his leg.

Explain why the athlete could find it difficult to run. [2 marks]

_____

_____

7 The diagram shows the biceps and triceps muscles in the upper arm.

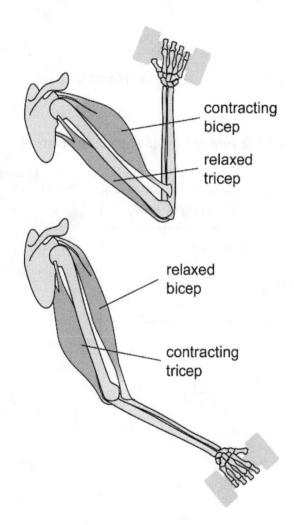

contracting bicep

relaxed tricep

relaxed bicep

contracting tricep

Use the diagram to describe how the muscles work together to straighten the arm. [2 marks]

_____

_____

_____

8 A handgrip dynamometer is an instrument that is used to test the strength of muscles in the forearm and hand.

A scientist uses the handgrip dynamometer to measure the force exerted by the muscles in the rock climber's hand and forearm muscles.

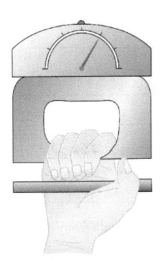

One measurement was taken at the end of each week, for 6 weeks.

Week	1	2	3	4	5	6
Force (N)	56.3	57.1	58.0	58.7	47.2	47.0

a. In which week did the rock climber have the strongest grip? **[1 mark]**

Week _____

b. Describe how the rock climber's forearm and hand strength changed over the 6 weeks. **[1 mark]**

_____

c. The rock climber injured herself during the 6 weeks.

Use the results to determine when the injury was most likely to have happened.

Explain your answer. **[2 marks]**

_____

_____

Total marks _____ /16

Biology – Organisms: cells to systems

1 Draw **one** line to match each word with the correct definition.

[2 marks]

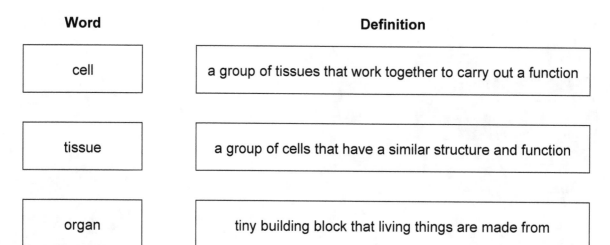

Word	Definition
cell	a group of tissues that work together to carry out a function
tissue	a group of cells that have a similar structure and function
organ	tiny building block that living things are made from

2 Which of the following is an example of an organ system that is found in the human body?

Circle **one** term.

[1 mark]

the brain   **the circulatory system**   **the lungs**   **the heart**

3 The diagram shows a cell.

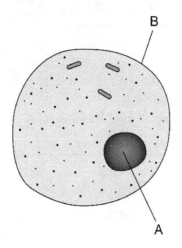

    a. Name the structures labelled **A** and **B**.

[2 marks]

        A _____

        B _____

    b. Describe the function of the structure labelled **A**.

[1 mark]

_____

4 The diagram shows a bacterium. Bacteria are too small to be seen by the naked eye.

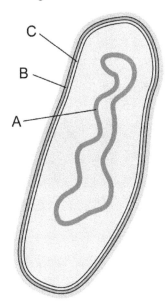

a. Identify the letter showing the structure that gives the bacterial cell its shape. **[1 mark]**

_____

b. Bacteria can absorb nutrients from their environment by diffusion. Identify the letter that shows the structure where nutrients are absorbed into the bacterium. **[1 mark]**

_____

c. Name the instrument that a scientist would need to use to view a bacterium. **[1 mark]**

_____

5 A scientist is viewing a sample of cells of unknown origin under a light microscope. The diagram shows a biological drawing of the cells. The scientist claims the cells are from a plant.

Magnification ×450

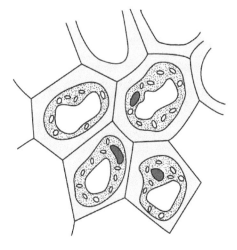

a. State **two** features of the cells that support the scientist's claim that they are plant cells. **[2 marks]**

1 _____

2 _____

b. To view the cells, the scientist used a stain called methylene blue.

Explain why the scientist used a stain. [1 mark]

_____

6 *Euglena* is a unicellular organism that sometimes forms a green scum on ponds. The diagram shows the structure of *Euglena*.

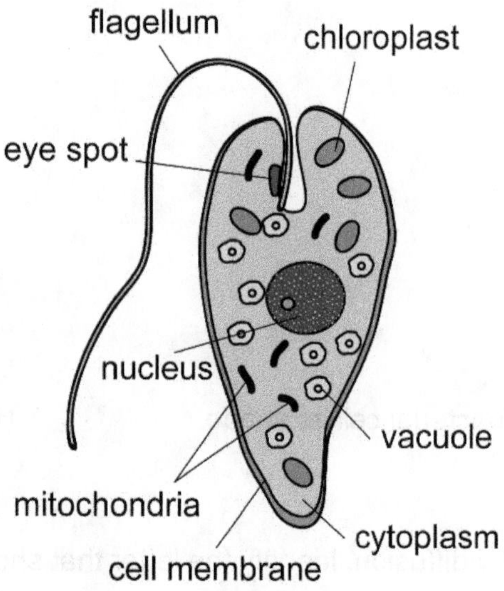

a. *Euglena* can use light from the Sun for photosynthesis.

Where does photosynthesis happen in *Euglena*?

Circle **one** term. [1 mark]

chloroplasts   **cell membrane**   **nucleus**   **membrane**

b. *Euglena* has a flagellum. The flagellum is like a tail.

Suggest how the flagellum helps *Euglena* survive. [2 marks]

_____

_____

7 An amoeba is a unicellular organism. An amoeba has a membrane that allows the diffusion of substances in and out of the cell.

Which statement best explains why diffusion of substances across the membrane is needed for an amoeba to survive? Tick **one** box. [1 mark]

So the amoeba can absorb vital nutrients ☐

So the amoeba can reproduce ☐

So the amoeba can get rid of water ☐

To protect the amoeba from attack ☐

Total marks _____ /16

Biology – Organisms: cells to systems

1 The human body is made up from millions of cells.

   Circle **one** statement that best describes a cell.   [1 mark]

   a type of organ   a tiny living unit   a type of nerve   a tiny non-living block

2 The diagram shows a cell.

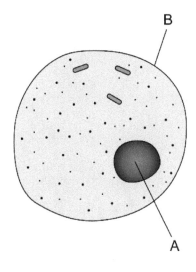

   Complete the table to show the names of the structures and the functions of parts **A** and **B**. [2 marks]

	Name of structure	Function
A		
B		

3 Which of the following flow diagrams best represents how organisms are organised?   [1 mark]

   Tick **one** box.

   a. | system > tissue > organ > cell | ☐

   b. | tissue > cell > organ | ☐

   c. | organ > tissue > system > cell | ☐

   d. | cell > tissue > organ > system | ☐

4 Describe the difference between a tissue and an organ. **[2 marks]**

_____

_____

5 A scientist is viewing a sample of cells of unknown origin under a light microscope. The diagram shows a biological drawing of the cells.

The scientist claims the cells are from a plant.

Magnification ×450

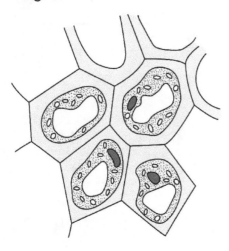

a. State **two** features of the cells that support the claim that they are plant cells. **[2 marks]**

1 _____

2 _____

b. To view the cells, the scientist used a stain called methylene blue.

Explain why the scientist used a stain. **[1 mark]**

_____

6 Draw **three** lines to match each part of a light microscope with its function. **[2 marks]**

Part	Function
eyepiece lens	the part you turn to produce a clear image
stage	the part you look through
focusing wheel	the flat surface where you put the slide

Biology – Organisms: cells to systems extended

7 *Euglena* is a unicellular organism that sometimes forms a green scum on ponds. The diagram shows the structure of *Euglena*.

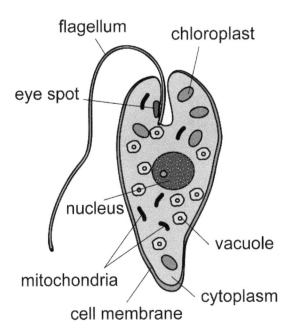

a. Name one feature of *Euglena* that suggests it is able to carry out photosynthesis.   **[1 mark]**

_____

b. *Euglena* has a flagellum.

Explain how a flagellum helps *Euglena* survive.   **[2 marks]**

_____

_____

8 Amoeba is a unicellular organism. An amoeba has a membrane that allows the diffusion of substances in and out of the cell.

Explain why diffusion of substances across the membrane is needed for amoeba to survive.   **[2 marks]**

_____

_____

Total marks _____ /16

Biology – Organisms: cells to systems extended

Biology – Ecosystems and habitats

1   The figure below shows four living things from a grassland habitat.

snake

grass

hawk

grasshopper

Not to scale

a.   Complete the food chain using the names of the organisms shown in the diagram.   **[1 mark]**

grass → _____ → _____ → _____

b.   Name the producer in this food chain.   **[1 mark]**

_____

c.   Explain what would happen to the number of hawks if the number of snakes decreased.   **[2 marks]**

_____

2   The diagram below shows a food web in a pond.

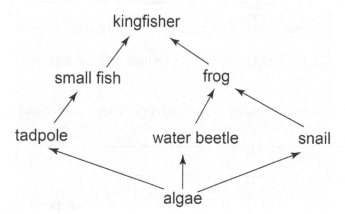

The number of small fish in this food web declines due to an increase in fishing.

Predict what will happen to the size of the population of algae.

Give a reason for your answer.   **[2 marks]**

_____

_____

3 The graph below shows how the population of bees changed in an area of the UK between 1947 and 2014.

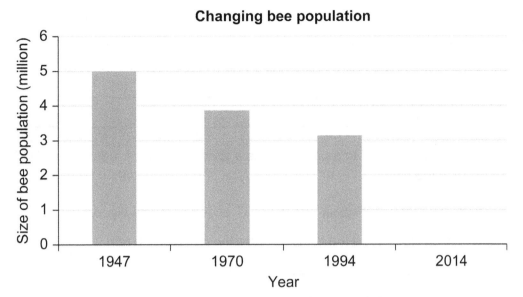

Changing bee population

a. In 2014 the population of bees was 2.5 million.

Complete the graph to show the population of bees in 2014. **[1 mark]**

b. Describe the trend shown in the graph. **[1 mark]**

_____

c. Which two of the following could explain why the population of bees has changed in this way?

Tick **two** boxes. **[2 marks]**

A decrease in parasites that kill bees ☐

An increase in use of pesticides ☐

A loss of habitat ☐

A decrease in fertiliser use ☐

Biology – Ecosystems and habitats core

4 The mammee apple depends on pollination by bees. Pollination happens when the pollen from a male plant fertilises the female plant to create a seed. The mammee apple fruit then develops around the seed.

Explain what would happen to the number of mammee apples produced if the bee population suddenly decreased. **[2 marks]**

_____

_____

5 A farmer sprays DDT on a field next to a pond. DDT is a toxic chemical. A week later DDT is detected in the algae in the pond.

a. Tick **two** statements that best explain how the DDT ended up in the algae. **[2 marks]**

The chemical was washed off the fields and into the pond by the rain. ☐

The chemical was absorbed by the weeds in the field. ☐

The chemical was absorbed by the algae roots in the pond. ☐

The algae ate the weeds. ☐

b. A month later several large fish that had been living in the pond were found dead on the surface of the water. Scientists found very high concentrations of DDT in the fish.

Explain how the large fish could have such high levels of DDT. **[2 marks]**

_____

_____

Total marks _____ /16

Biology – Ecosystems and habitats

1 Draw **one** line to match each word with the correct meaning.   **[2 marks]**

Word   **Definition**

| habitat |

| all the members of a single species that live in a habitat |

| population |

| all the conditions that surround a living organism |

| environment |

| the place where an organism lives |

2 Complete the sentences. Choose from these words.   **[2 marks]**

consumer   energy   food   oxygen   predator   producer   water

A food chain shows what eats what in a habitat. It also shows how _____ flows through organisms living in a habitat. Food chains start with a _____.

3 The diagram below shows a food web in a pond.

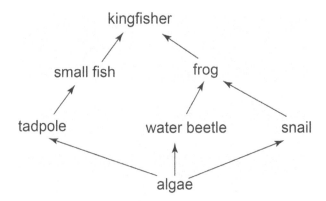

All the frogs in the food web die of a disease.

Explain what will happen to the size of the population of snails.   **[2 marks]**

_____

_____

4 The graph below shows how the population of bees changed in an area of the UK between 1947 and 2014.

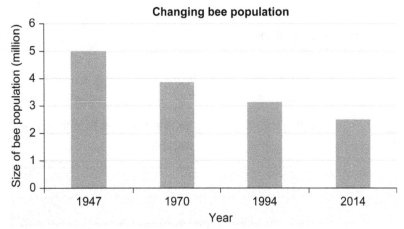

Changing bee population

a. Between 1947 and 2014, what was the overall decrease in the bee population? **[1 mark]**

_____ million

b. Suggest **one** reason why the population of bees has changed. **[1 mark]**

_____

c. The mammee apple depends on pollination by bees. Pollination happens when the pollen from a male plant fertilises the female plant to create a seed. The mammee apple fruit then develops around the seed.

Explain what would happen to the number of mammee apples produced if the bee population decreased dramatically. **[2 marks]**

_____

_____

5 Lynx are predators of the snowshoe hares. The graph shows how the estimated population of snowshoe hares and lynx in one part of Canada changed over 20 years.

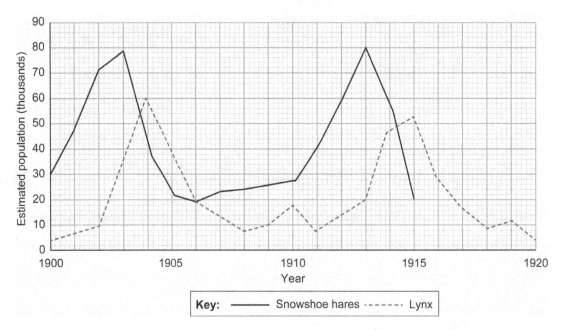

Key: —— Snowshoe hares - - - - - - Lynx

Year	1916	1917	1918	1919	1920
Estimated number of snowshoe hares (thousands)	28	16	9	12	5

a. Use the data in the table to finish plotting the line for the snowshoe hares. **[1 mark]**

b. When the snowshoe hare population increased, the lynx population also started to increase.

Explain why. **[2 marks]**

_____

_____

6 A scientist is investigating the accumulation of mercury in an ocean food chain. In this food chain plankton is the producer and tuna is the top predator.

The results are shown in the table.

Organism	Concentration of mercury (arbitrary units)
tuna	30
large fish	10
small fish	3
plankton	1

Explain why the tuna fish have the highest concentration of mercury. **[3 marks]**

_____

_____

_____

Total marks _____ /16

Biology – Ecosystems and habitats extended

Biology – Plant reproduction

1 The diagram below shows the parts of a flower.

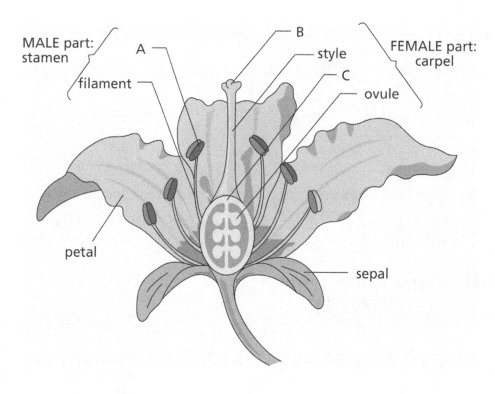

MALE part:
stamen

FEMALE part:
carpel

A

B

style

C

ovule

filament

petal

sepal

a. State the letter of the label that shows the ovary. **[1 mark]**

_____

b. State the letter of the label that shows the stigma. **[1 mark]**

_____

c. State the letter of the label that shows the structure that produces pollen. **[1 mark]**

_____

2 Complete the sentences. Choose from these words. **[2 marks]**

seed   **nectar**   **ovary**   **oxygen**   **pollen**   **sperm**

In pollination, _____ is transferred from the male part of a flower to the female part
of a flower. After fertilisation a _____ is formed.

3 Lavender plants are pollinated by insects.

Explain how insects can pollinate lavender plants. **[2 marks]**

_____

_____

4 Which statement best describes fertilisation in plants?

Tick **one** box.

[1 mark]

The ovule and pollen cell meet. ☐

The anther and stigma meet. ☐

The ovary ripens. ☐

The pollen and stigma meet. ☐

5 *Passiflora edulis* is a plant that produces passion fruit, which are sweet and juicy.

The fruit contains many seeds.

Explain how the seeds of the passion flower are dispersed. [2 marks]

_____

_____

6 Oliver has three different seeds, each with a different shape. He investigates which seed will travel the furthest distance in the wind.

Oliver drops each seed from a height of 2.5 metres and measures how far each one travels. He uses a fan to produce air movement like the wind.

Seed	Distance travelled (cm)			Average distance (cm)
A	236	189	210	212
B	86	75	102	88
C	20	34	12	

a. Complete the table by calculating the mean (average) distance travelled by **C**. [1 mark]

b. Which seed is most likely to be dispersed by the wind?

Explain your answer. [2 marks]

_____

c. What was the independent variable in Oliver's investigation?

Tick **one** box.

[1 mark]

The distance travelled by the seed ☐

The type of seed ☐

The height the seed was dropped from ☐

The colour of the seed ☐

7   The concentration of sugar affects how well pollen tubes grow.

Khadija uses different concentrations of sugar solution and counts the number of pollen tubes that grow in each solution. Her results are shown in the bar chart.

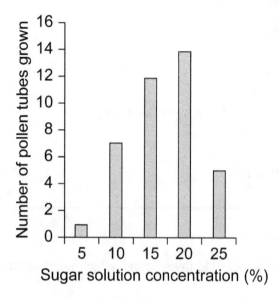

Khadija concludes that 'increasing the sugar concentration increases the number of pollen tubes that grow'.

Do Khadija's results support her conclusion?

Use evidence from the graph in your answer.   **[2 marks]**

_____

_____

Total marks _____ /16

Biology – Plant reproduction

1   The diagram below shows the parts of a flower.

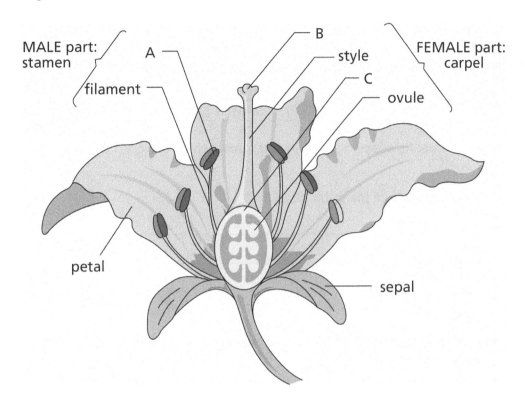

MALE part: stamen

A

filament

B

style

C

ovule

FEMALE part: carpel

petal

sepal

Name the stuctures labelled **A** and **B**.

A _____ [1 mark]

B _____ [1 mark]

2   The flower is the site of pollination. Describe what happens in pollination. **[2 marks]**

_____

3   **a.** Emily sees an article about growing strawberries in a gardening magazine.

A tip reads 'to increase the number of strawberry fruits use a paint brush and gently tickle the inside of each flower'.

Explain how following this tip could result in more strawberry fruit. **[2 marks]**

_____

_____

b. Strawberry flowers contain nectar.

Explain how this helps increase the chances of pollination. **[2 marks]**

_____

_____

4 The statements in the table describe the different stages leading up to fertilisation in a plant.

Write numbers **1–4** to show the correct order of stages. The first one has been done for you. **[1 mark]**

Pollen cell lands on female part of plant.	1
A pollen tube grows out of the pollen cell.	
The nucleus of the pollen cell meets the nucleus of an ovule.	
Pollen tube grows until it meets the ovary.	

5 Witch hazel is a type of tree. Its seeds develop in small pods which explode, dispersing the seeds away from the tree.

Explain why this is an advantage to the witch hazel plant. **[2 marks]**

_____

_____

6 Oliver has three different seeds, each with a different shape. He investigates which seed will travel the furthest distance in the wind.

He drops each seed from a height of 2.5 metres and measures how far each one travels. He uses a fan to produce air movement like the wind.

Seed	Distance travelled (cm)			Average distance (cm)
A	236	189	210	212
B	86	75	102	88
C	20	34	12	

a. Complete the table by calculating the mean distance travelled by seed **C**. **[1 mark]**

b. Which seed is most likely to be dispersed by the wind?

Explain your answer. **[2 marks]**

_____

Biology – Plant reproduction extended

7 The concentration of sugar affects how well pollen tubes grow.

Khadija uses different concentrations of sugar solution and counts the number of pollen tubes that grow in each solution. Her results are shown in the table.

Concentration of sugar solution (%)	Average length of pollen tube (µm)
5	149
10	242
15	334
20	71

Khadija concludes that 'increasing the sugar concentration increases the number of pollen tubes that grow'.

Do Khadija's results support her conclusion? Use evidence from the table in your answer.   **[2 marks]**

_____

_____

Total marks _____ **/16**

Biology – Variation

1 The pictures below show two types of pony.

a. Describe one similarity in the characteristics of the two ponies.   **[1 mark]**

_____

b. Describe one difference in the characteristics of the two ponies.   **[1 mark]**

_____

c. What name is given to a group of living organisms that have similar features?   **[1 mark]**

Tick **one** box.

A gene   ☐

A kingdom   ☐

A species   ☐

An order   ☐

2 State the term given to describe the differences in the characteristics found within a species. **[1 mark]**

_____

3 Complete the sentences. Choose from these words.   **[2 marks]**

continuous   class   discontinuous   gradual   less   more

A characteristic such as height changes gradually. This is known as _____
variation.

A characteristic such eye colour has a distinct range of categories. This is known as
_____ variation.

4 Draw **one** line from each characteristic to the correct type of data.   **[4 marks]**

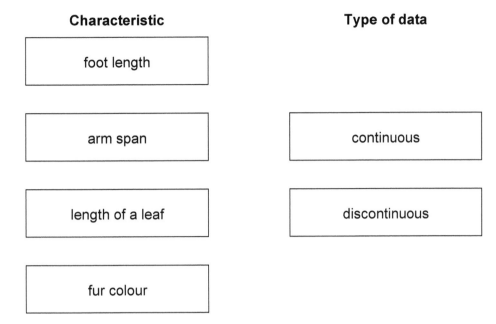

Characteristic	Type of data
foot length	
arm span	continuous
length of a leaf	discontinuous
fur colour	

5 Scientists can classify human blood as being one of four different types. These are known as blood groups. A scientist investigates the number of people with different blood groups. Her results are shown in the table.

Name of blood group	Number of people with the blood group
AB	5
A	40
O	50
B	10

a. Complete the bar chart to show the data in the table. [2 marks]

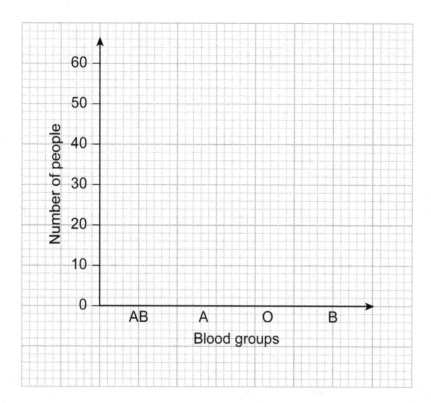

b. Which was the most common blood group?

_____ [1 mark]

c. What causes different people to have different blood groups? [1 mark]

_____

6 A student collects some data on the variation in ear lobes in his class. His results are shown in the table.

Type of ear lobe	Number of students
attached lobe	4
unattached lobe	10

In the UK, 99 per cent of the population has unattached earlobes. Explain why the data collected by the student is not representative of the population. [2 marks]

_____

_____

Total marks _____ /16

Biology – Variation

1 The diagrams below show three different organisms.

   a. Describe one physical characteristic that all the organisms have in common.   **[1 mark]**

_____

   b. Describe one physical characteristic that is unique to the elephant.   **[1 mark]**

_____

2 Which statement best describes a species?

Tick **one** box.   **[1 mark]**

Organisms that are able to reproduce ☐

Organisms that all have exactly the same characteristics ☐

Organisms with similar characteristics that reproduce together to give fertile offspring ☐

Organisms with similar characteristics that cannot reproduce together ☐

3 Describe what is meant by the term *variation*?   **[1 mark]**

_____

4 Complete the following sentences. Choose from these words.   **[2 marks]**

     continuous   **class**   **discontinuous**   **gradual**   **less**   **more**

A characteristic that changes gradually is called _____ variation.

A characteristic that has a distinct range of options or categories is called
_____variation.

5 Draw **one** line to match each characteristic to the correct type of data. **[3 marks]**

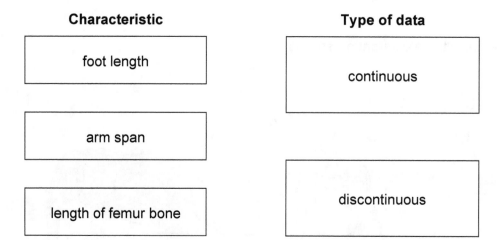

Characteristic	Type of data

6 Scientists can classify human blood as being one of four different types. These are known as blood groups.

A scientist investigates the number of people with different blood groups. Her results are shown in the table.

Name of blood group	Number of people with the blood group
AB	5
A	40
O	50
B	10

Biology – Variation extended

a. Construct a graph or chart to show the data in the table.   **[3 marks]**

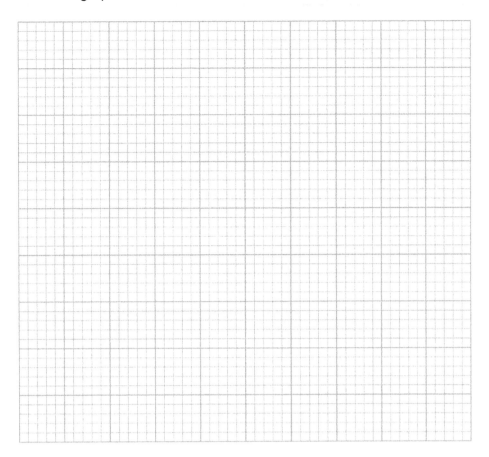

b. Name the two blood groups that were the most common blood groups in the sample.   **[1 mark]**

_____

c. What causes different people to have different blood groups?   **[1 mark]**

_____

7 A student collects some data on the variation in ear lobes in his class.

His results are shown in the table.

Type of ear lobe	Number of students
attached lobe	4
unattached lobe	10

In the UK, 99% of the population has unattached earlobes. Explain why the data collected by the student is not representative of the population.   **[2 marks]**

_____

_____

_____

Total marks _____ /16

Biology – Variation extended

Biology – Human reproduction

1 The diagram shows the female reproductive system.

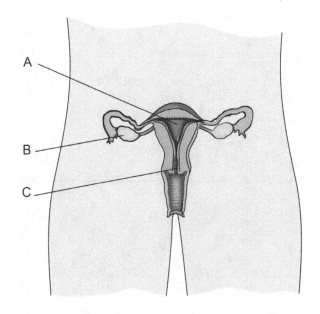

a. Name the structure labelled **A** in the diagram. [1 mark]

_____

b. Name the structure labelled **B** in the diagram. [1 mark]

_____

c. Which letter shows the structure where a foetus develops? [1 mark]

_____

2 Draw **one** line from each word to the correct definition. [2 marks]

Word	Definition
ovulation	the period of development of a foetus from fertilised egg to birth
fertilisation	the joining of the nucleus of an egg and a sperm cell
gestation	the release of eggs

3 Sperm are the male sex cells in humans. What is the general name for a sex cell?   [1 mark]

Tick **one** box.

zygote ☐

embryo ☐

gamete ☐

nucleus ☐

4 Describe one function of the testes.   [1 mark]

_____

5 The graph shows changes to the thickness of the uterus lining in a female with a 28-day cycle.

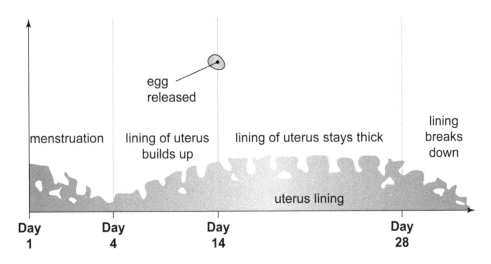

Use the graph to answer the questions.

a. On what day of the cycle does the uterus lining begin to build up?   [1 mark]

_____

b. On what day of the cycle does ovulation occur for this woman?   [1 mark]

_____

6 During pregnancy the placenta allows substances to pass between the foetus and mother. The mother's blood does not mix with the blood of the foetus, but the placenta lets substances pass between the two blood supplies.

Complete the table by adding ticks to show which way the substances pass.   [3 marks]

Substance	Passes from mother's blood to foetus' blood	Passes from foetus' blood to mother's blood
oxygen		
carbon dioxide		
glucose		

7 A woman has just become pregnant. Her doctor advises her not to drink alcohol during her pregnancy.

Explain why. **[2 marks]**

_____

_____

8 Some scientists carried out an investigation into the effects of smoking during pregnancy on the birth mass of babies.

The table shows the scientist's results.

Average number of cigarettes smoked by pregnant woman each day	Average birth mass of baby (grams)
0	3500
10	3460
20	3410
30	3340
40	3255

a. Calculate the difference in average birth mass of the babies of the mothers that did not smoke and the mothers that smoked 40 cigarettes each day. **[1 mark]**

_____

b. What conclusion can be drawn from the data? **[1 mark]**

_____

Total marks _____ /16

Biology – Human reproduction

1 The diagram shows the female reproductive system.

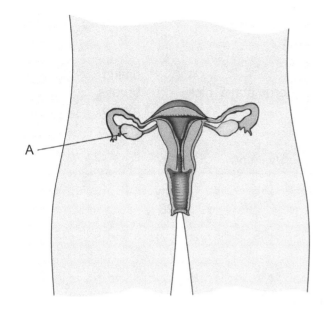

A

   a. Name the structure labelled **A** in the diagram. [1 mark]

   _____

   b What is the function of this structure? [1 mark]

   _____

   c. Add a label to the diagram to show an oviduct. [1 mark]

2 Sperm is the male sex cell in humans. What is the general name for a sex cell? [1 mark]

   _____

3 Describe the difference between ovulation and fertilisation. [2 marks]

   _____

   _____

4 A man's testes are contained in a bag of skin called a scrotum. The scrotum hangs outside the body.

   Normal body temperature is 37°C. Suggest what temperature is best for sperm production.

   Tick **one** box. [1 mark]

   20°C ☐

   35–36°C ☐

   37°C ☐

   38–39°C ☐

5 The graph shows changes to the thickness of the uterus lining in a female with a 28-day cycle.

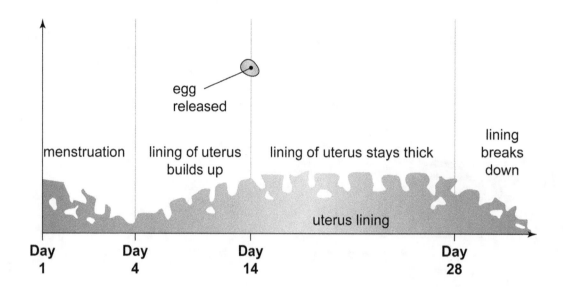

Use the graph to answer the questions.

a. On what day does the lining of the uterus begin to build up?   [1 mark]

_____

b. On which day in the cycle is this woman most likely to get pregnant?

Tick **one** box.   [1 mark]

Day 1   ☐

Day 4   ☐

Day 14   ☐

Day 28   ☐

c. Explain why the uterus lining stays thick between days 14 and 28.   [1 mark]

_____

6 A human foetus takes 38 weeks to grow from a fertilised cell into a baby that is ready to be born.

What is the name given to this period of development?   [1 mark]

_____

7 During pregnancy the placenta allows substances to pass between the foetus and mother. The mother's blood does not mix with the blood of the foetus, but the placenta lets substances pass between the two blood supplies.

Complete the table by adding ticks to show which way (if any) the substances pass.   **[3 marks]**

Substance	Passes from mother's blood to foetus' blood	Passes from foetus' blood to mother's blood	Does not pass between mother's blood and foetus' blood
oxygen			
carbon dioxide			
glucose			

8 Smoking in pregnancy is said to increase the risk of premature birth and low birth weight.

Identify two pieces of evidence that support this claim.

Tick **two** boxes.   **[2 marks[**

A study of 900 children showed that children of mothers who smoked in pregnancy were three times more likely to develop asthma than non-smoking mothers.

☐

Large-scale studies have shown that babies of mothers who smoked in pregnancy are about 150–200 g lighter at birth.

☐

A study of 4500 mothers found that smokers had a 40 per cent higher risk of premature birth compared with non-smokers.

☐

A study of 20 mothers showed that babies of mothers who smoked 0–5 cigarettes per week did not have a significantly increased risk of premature birth.

☐

Total marks _____ /16

Chemistry – The particulate nature of matter

core

1   The diagram shows the arrangement of particles in the three different states: solid, liquid, gas.

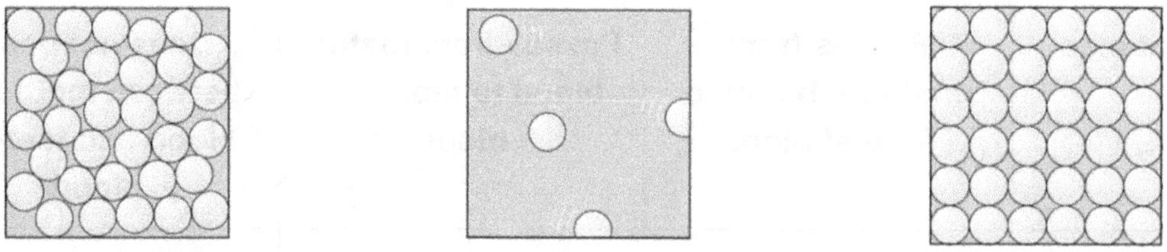

_____   _____   _____

   a.   Label each diagram.   **[3 marks]**

   b.   A student is drinking a cup of milk.

        Describe how the arrangement of particles in the cup differs from the arrangement of
particles in the milk.   **[2 marks]**

        _____

        _____

   c.   A gas can be compressed but solids and liquids cannot.

        Explain why.   **[2 marks]**

        _____

        _____

2   Draw **one** line from each word to the correct definition.   **[3 marks]**

Word	Definition
subliming	liquid to solid
condensing	solid to gas
evaporating	liquid to gas
freezing	gas to liquid

3 An ice cube was put into a glass of orange juice.

After 10 minutes the ice cube had melted.

a. Describe how the ice cube changed during the 10 minutes.   **[2 marks]**

_____

_____

b. Complete the diagram to show how the arrangement of particles in the ice cube changed
during the 10 minutes.   **[1 mark]**

4 Two friends were shopping in town. When they passed the bakery they could smell freshly
baked bread, which started to make them hungry.

a. Name the process by which 'smells' spread out.

Circle **one** term.   **[1 mark]**

   evaporation   **density**   **diffusion**   **boiling**

b. Suggest a reason why they could smell the bread out in the street.   **[1 mark]**

_____

_____

c. Predict what will happen to the smell of bread as they walk away from the shop.   **[1 mark]**

_____

_____

Total marks _____ /16

Chemistry – The particulate nature of matter

1   The diagrams show a diamond, some golden syrup being poured onto a spoon and an aerosol deodorant.

    a. Compare **one** physical property of diamond with that of golden syrup.   **[1 mark]**

_____

_____

    b. Describe how the particles are arranged in the diamond.   **[1 mark]**

_____

    c. Explain why golden syrup is runny.   **[2 marks]**

_____

_____

    d. Explain why the gas pressure decreases in the can as the deodorant is used up.   **[2 marks]**

_____

_____

2   Complete the diagram.   **[2 marks]**

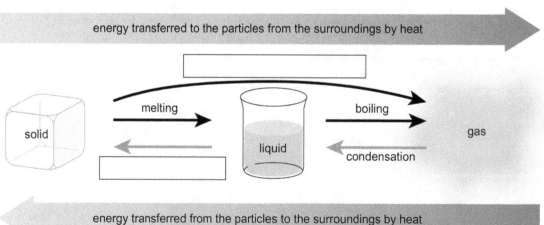

3 Two friends were shopping in town. When they passed the bakery they could smell freshly baked bread, which started to make them hungry.

   a. Name the process by which 'smells' spread out.

   Circle **one** term.   [1 mark]

        evaporation   density   diffusion   boiling

   b. Suggest a reason why they could smell the bread out in the street.   [1 mark]

   _____

   _____

   c. Predict what will happen to the smell of bread as they walk away from the shop. [1 mark]

   _____

   _____

4 The table lists the melting points and boiling points of some substances.

Substance	Melting point (°C)	Boiling point (°C)
water	0	100
tin	232	2602
mercury	−39	357
ethanol	−114	78
salt	801	1413
helium	−272	−268

   a. Name a substance that is in the liquid state at 20°C.   [1 mark]

   _____

   b. Name a substance that is in the solid state at 20°C.   [1 mark]

   _____

   c. Helium is a gas at 20°C. Use the data in the table to explain why.   [2 marks]

   _____

   _____

   d. Explain why salt has a higher melting point than tin.   [1 mark]

   _____

   Total marks _____ /16

Chemistry – The particulate nature of matter extended

Chemistry – Pure and impure substances

`core`

1 a. Complete the following sentences. Choose from these words. [4 marks]

> **one   two   chemically   physically   pure   impure**

A _____ substance contains only _____ type of particle.

A mixture is made up of at least _____ pure substances that are not _____ joined together.

b. Identify the mixture in the list below. Circle **one** term. [1 mark]

> **distilled water   gold   milk   oxygen gas**

c. Suggest a reason why mineral water is not pure. [1 mark]

_____

2 a. Draw **one** line from **each** diagram to its separation process. [3 marks]

Diagram	Process

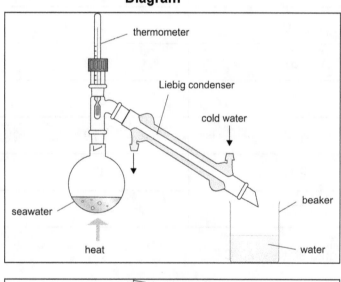

chromatography

distillation

evaporation

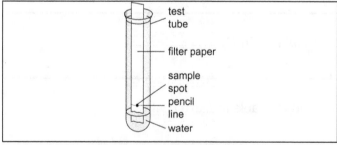

filtration

crystallisation

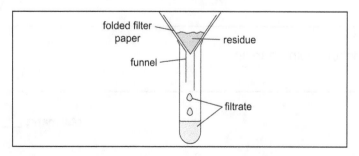

b. A student wants to separate a mixture of ethanol and water.

Name the process he should use. Give a reason for your answer. **[2 marks]**

_____

_____

3 The following processes are used to obtain pure salt from rock salt.

    evaporating   dissolving   crystallising   filtering

a. Write the processes in the correct order. **[3 marks]**

    1 _____

    2 _____

    3 _____

    4 _____

b. Explain how filtration works. **[2 marks]**

_____

_____

Total marks _____ /16

Chemistry – Pure and impure substances

1 A group of students are investigating the solubility of potassium nitrate at different temperatures. Their results are shown in the graph.

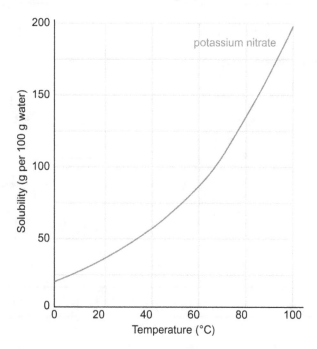

a. Write down the independent variable. [1 mark]

_____

b. Write down the dependent variable. [1 mark]

_____

c. Identify a variable that must be controlled. [1 mark]

_____

d. Describe what you would see if 60 g of potassium nitrate was added to 100 g of water at 20°C. [1 mark]

_____

e. Determine the relationship between the solubility of potassium nitrate and temperature. [1 mark]

_____

f. Use your ideas about particles to explain what happens when potassium nitrate dissolves in water. [2 marks]

_____

_____

_____

2 The diagram shows the chromatogram obtained by a group of students investigating food colouring in a range of different sweets.

1 2 3 4

a. Write down the number of substances found in sweet 1.   [1 mark]

_____

b. Explain how you know one substance is found in all the sweets.   [1 mark]

_____

c. Explain how chromatography works.   [2 marks]

_____

_____

_____

_____

3 The diagram shows the equipment used to carry out simple distillation.

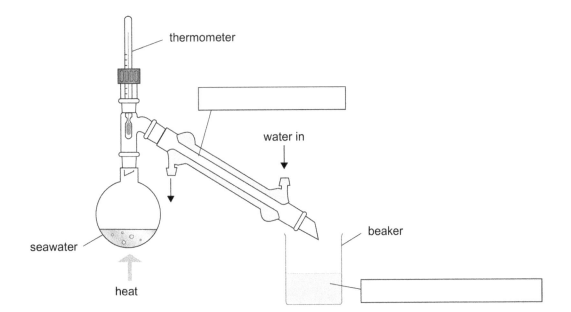

thermometer

water in

beaker

seawater

heat

a. Label the diagram. [2 marks]

b. Explain how distillation works.

Use your ideas about particle theory in your answer. [3 marks]

_____

_____

_____

_____

Total marks _____ /16

Chemistry – Pure and impure substances extended

Chemistry – Acids and alkalis

core

1 a. Draw **one** line from each word to the correct definition.   [3 marks]

Word	Definition

Word

indicator

base

acid

Definition

has pH below 7

has pH above 7

is used to identify whether a solution is acidic or alkaline

is a substance that neutralises an acid

b. Acids and alkalis can be corrosive or irritants.

Identify the hazard symbols often found on acidic substances.

Tick **two** boxes.   [1 mark]

c. Write down **one** safety precaution you should take when handling acids.   [1 mark]

_____

The chemical formulae for four acids are shown in the table.

Hydrochloric acid	Nitric acid	Sulfuric acid	Ethanoic acid
HCl	HNO_3	H_2SO_4	CH_3COOH

d. Identify the element present in **all** of the acids.   [1 mark]

_____

2 The strength of an acid is measured using the pH scale.

The diagram shows how the colour of universal indicator changes at different pHs.

a. Label the diagram.   [3 marks]

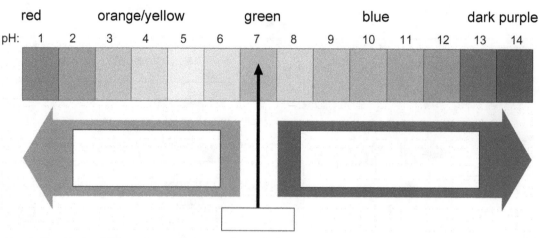

b. Complete the table. The first row has been done for you.   [2 marks]

Substance	pH	Acid or alkali?
hydrochloric acid	0–1	strong acid
hand soap	8	_____
oven cleaner	12	_____

c. Explain the advantage of using universal indicator over red cabbage indicator.   [2 marks]

_____

_____

3 A student is playing with his friends in the garden when his arm is stung by a wasp.

Wasp stings are slightly alkaline.

His friend puts some vinegar onto the sting.

Soon the student's arm starts to feel a bit better.

a. Estimate the pH of the vinegar. Circle **one** number.   [1 mark]

    1   3   7   9

b. Explain why the student's arm started to feel better.   [2 marks]

_____

_____

Total marks _____ /16

Chemistry – Acids and alkalis core

Chemistry – Acids and alkalis

1   A group of students used a pH sensor to investigate how the pH changed during a chemical reaction.

They measured out 10 cm³ of hydrochloric acid and poured it into a small beaker.

They recorded the pH before adding sodium hydroxide.

a.   Name the type of reaction they were investigating.

Circle **one** term.   [1 mark]

   displacement   **neutralisation**   **acidic**   **physical**

b.   Complete the word equation for the reaction.   [1 mark]

   hydrochloric acid + sodium hydroxide → _____ + _____

The results are recorded in the table.

Volume of alkali added (cm³)	pH of mixture
0.0	1.0
1.0	1.0
2.0	1.0
3.0	2.5
4.0	5.0
5.0	7.0
6.0	9.0
7.0	9.5
8.0	9.5
9.0	9.5
10.0	9.5

c. Plot the data points on the axes below. [2 marks]

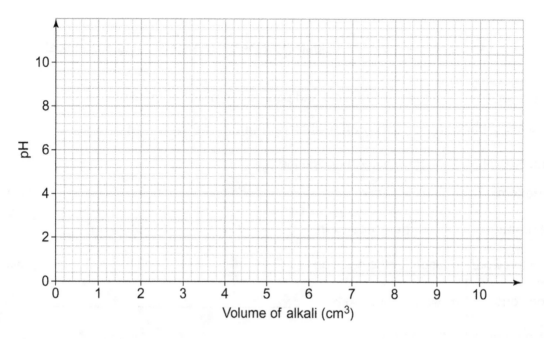

d. Draw a smooth curve on the graph. [1 mark]

Look at the graph.

e. Describe the shape of the graph. [2 marks]

_____

_____

f. Suggest a reason why the pH does not increase higher than 9.5. [1 mark]

_____

_____

2 Three pairs of chemicals are listed below.

Draw **one** line from each reaction to the correct result. [2 marks]

Pair of chemicals	Result
magnesium + hydrochloric acid	a chloride and water are formed
copper + sulfuric acid	a chloride and hydrogen gas are formed
potassium hydroxide + hydrochloric acid	no reaction

3 A science class is learning about tooth decay. Here are hypotheses from **two** of the students.

Student A: Sugar causes tooth decay.

Student B: Acid causes tooth decay.

The students carried out an investigation in which they used egg shells to represent teeth.

The students set up the following test tubes and recorded the pH of each solution.

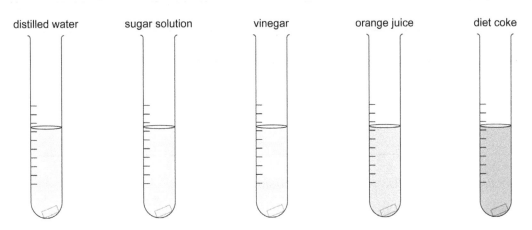

a. Write down **one** variable that the students must control. [1 mark]

_____

b. Suggest a reason why the first tube contained distilled water. [1 mark]

_____

c. Explain why the students measured the pH. [1 mark]

_____

After 5 days the students recorded their observations in the table.

Substance	pH	Observation after 5 days
distilled water	7.0	no change
sugar solution	7.0	no change
vinegar	2.5	the egg shell has disappeared
orange juice	4.1	the egg was pitted
diet coke	3.2	the egg shell was really thin

d. Use the observations to determine which hypothesis was correct. [3 marks]

_____

_____

_____

Total marks _____ /16

Chemistry – Acids and alkalis extended

Chemistry – Chemical reactions of metals and non-metals

1 a. Compare the physical properties of a plastic spoon with those of a metal spoon. **[3 marks]**

_____

_____

_____

b. Large cooking spoons are often made from metal but have plastic handles.

Explain why. **[1 mark]**

_____

_____

2 The image shows some wood burning in a combustion reaction.

Complete the following sentences.

Choose from these terms. **[3 marks]**

liquid	carbon	oxygen	displacement	hydrogen	water

gas	thermal decompostion	oxidation

Combustion is a special example of an _____ reaction. Fuels such as wood contain the element carbon. During the reaction carbon reacts with _____ in the air to form carbon dioxide. This _____ escapes into the atmosphere.

3 When copper is heated it reacts with a gas in the air.

a. Name the gas. **[1 mark]**

_____

b. Complete the word equation for the reaction. **[2 marks]**

copper + _____ → _____

c. Identify the statement that describes what happens in a **chemical change** but is not a **physical change**.

Tick **one** box. [1 mark]

Mass is conserved during the reaction. ☐

The product is a gas. ☐

The particles have combined in different ways to make a new substance. ☐

The changes take place at high temperatures. ☐

4 A group of students were investigating the reaction of sulfuric acid with metals.

The results are recorded in the table.

Metal	Observations when sulfuric acid is added
copper	no change
magnesium	vigorous bubbles
zinc	lots of bubbles
cobalt	a few bubbles

a. Determine the order of reactivity of the metals.

Write them in order from the most reactive to the least reactive. [1 mark]

_____

b. Justify your answer to part **a**. [1 mark]

_____

c. Complete the word equation. [2 marks]

magnesium + sulfuric acid → _____ + _____

d. The students decided to repeat the experiment but this time they used nitric acid.

Predict how the metals will react. [1 mark]

_____

Total marks _____ /16

Chemistry – Chemical reactions of metals and non-metals core

Chemistry – Chemical reactions of metals and non-metals

1   A teacher mixed some grey iron filings with the yellow non-metal sulfur in a tray.

    She then held a magnet near the mixture.

    a.   Describe what happened next.

         Give a reason for your answer.   [2 marks]

    _____

    _____

    _____

    b.   When the mixture was heated it glowed and a black solid was made.

         Write down a piece of evidence that shows a chemical reaction has taken place.   [1 mark]

    _____

2   A student is investigating the reaction between an iron nail and copper sulfate solution.

    The image shows the nail and solution at the start of the investigation and then 1 week later.

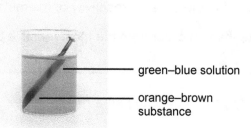

    a.   Describe the changes that have taken place during the reaction.   [2 marks]

    _____

    _____

    b.   Name the orange–brown coloured metal that has formed during the reaction.   [1 mark]

    _____

    c.   Particle diagrams can be used to represent the chemical change taking place.

         Complete the particle diagram for this reaction.   [1 mark]

 + → + _____

d. Identify the type of reaction that has taken place. [1 mark]

Tick **one** box.

Neutralisation ☐

Oxidation ☐

Displacement ☐

Combustion ☐

The student pours some of the green–blue solution into a test tube and adds some pieces of copper metal.

e. Predict what will happen. Give a reason for your answer. [2 marks]

_____

_____

Part of the reactivity series of metals is shown below.

Increasing reactivity

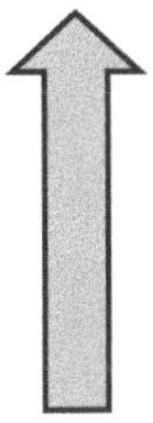

Potassium
Sodium
Calcium
Aluminium
Zinc
Lead

f. Use the information given in the reactivity series.

Identify **two** metals that would **not react** with aluminium nitrate.

Circle **two** words. [2 marks]

    zinc   potassium   lead   calcium   sodium

3 Two students heated solid copper carbonate in a crucible and a thermal decomposition reaction took place.

They recorded their observations in the table below.

	At the start	After heating
Colour of copper carbonate	green	black
Mass of crucible and copper carbonate	10 g	6.6 g

a. Explain the colour change that has taken place. [1 mark]

_____

b. Calculate the change in mass of the crucible and the solid after heating. [1 mark]

_____

c. Suggest a reason why the mass of the solid has decreased. [1 mark]

_____

d. A student repeats the experiment using a crucible containing the same amount of solid sodium carbonate.

Predict what would happen to the mass of the crucible and the solid substance after heating.

Circle **one** answer. [1 mark]

Mass will increase   **Mass will stay the same**   **Mass will decrease**

Total marks _____ /16

Chemistry – Earth and rocks

1 The diagram shows the structure of the Earth.

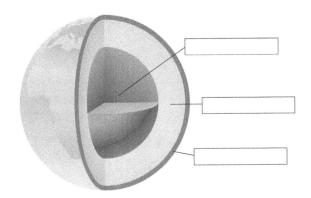

a. Label the diagram.

Choose from these terms. [3 marks]

igneous   **mantle**   **crust**   **core**   **lithosphere**   **metamorphic**

b. Draw **one** line from each term to the correct definition. [2 marks]

Word	Definition
igneous rock	formed from layers of sediment, often contains fossils
metamorphic rock	formed from cooling magma above or below the surface
sedimentary rock	formed by intense heat and pressure on other rocks

2 Diorite and dacite are both igneous rocks. They are shown in the images below.

diorite

dacite

a. Describe **one** difference between the rocks. [1 mark]

_____

b. Explain your answer to part **a**. [2 marks]

_____

_____

c. In Neolithic times dacite was used to make axes.

Suggest a reason why. [2 marks]

_____

_____

3 a. Fossils are often seen in patios made from sandstone, which is a sedimentary rock.

Explain why. [2 marks]

_____

_____

_____

Two statues were put up in a park 100 years ago.

The statue on the left is made from limestone, a sedimentary rock. It looks old and crumbly.

The statue on the right is made from marble, a metamorphic rock. It still looks quite new.

b. Explain why the statues look different. [2 marks]

_____

_____

_____

Slate is often used as a building material by the construction industry. It is strong, waterproof and resistant to weather.

c. Suggest a reason why slate has these properties. [2 marks]

_____

_____

_____

Total marks _____ /16

Chemistry – Earth and rocks

1   Look at the diagram of the tectonic plates on the Earth's surface.

a.   Suggest a reason why tectonic plates are moving all the time.   [1 mark]

_____

b.   Describe what could happen when the plates crash into each other.   [1 mark]

_____

_____

c.   Describe how scientists study the centre of the Earth although they cannot see it.   [2 marks]

_____

_____

2   a.   Complete the following sentence.   [2 marks]

The Earth's rocks are continually changing because of processes such as

_____

_____

b.   Compare the process of erosion with the process of weathering.   [2 marks]

_____

_____

c.   A Space Rover is exploring the surface of a newly discovered planet.

Some images showing mountains and large piles of small rocks have been sent back
to Earth.

Predict what the climate might be like on this planet.

Give a reason for your answer.   [2 marks]

_____

_____

_____

3 The diagram below shows the rock cycle.

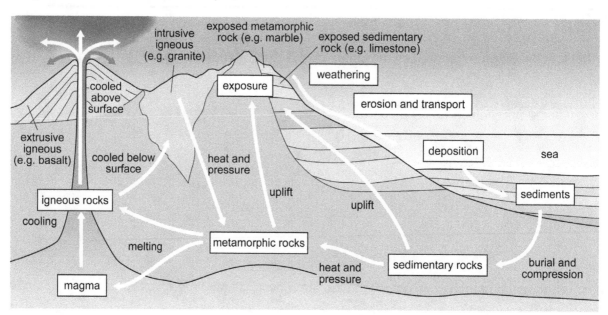

a. After millions of years, limestone rocks originally formed under the sea are converted into granite found in the mountains.

Use the diagram to describe how this happens. **[4 marks]**

_____

_____

_____

_____

b. Describe **one** difference between the rock cycle and a chemical reaction such as burning.

Thinking about changes of physical state, what would **one** similarity be? **[2 marks]**

_____

_____

_____

Total marks _____ /16

Chemistry – Dalton's atomic theory

core

1 Complete the following sentences.

Choose from these words. **[4 marks]**

compounds   elements   calculations   particles   atoms

molecules   experiments

The ancient Greeks believed that everything was made up of very tiny _____, called _____, and that they were all the same.

In 1803 Dalton proposed a new theory based on evidence from _____ and _____. Dalton now believed that not all atoms were the same but depended on the type of matter they were made from.

2 Some of Dalton's ideas are listed below.

- Atoms cannot be broken down into anything simpler.
- All the atoms of an element are the same.
- When two or more different types of atoms join together a compound is formed.
- During a chemical reaction atoms are rearranged.

a. Circle **two** compounds. **[2 marks]**

H_2 (diagram) CO_2 (diagram)

b. Look at the diagrams.

Identify the diagram that shows **one** element.

Tick **one** box. **[1 mark]**

A ☐   B ☐   C ☐

According to Dalton's theory, when an atom of hydrogen reacts with an atom of fluorine, a hydrogen fluoride molecule is formed.

c. Complete the particle equation.

Describe what happens to the atoms during the reaction. **[2 marks]**

◯ + ● → _____

_____

_____

3 The table lists some of the symbols used by Dalton.

Element	Symbol used by Dalton
hydrogen	⊙
oxygen	◯
carbon	⬤
sulfur	⊕
nitrogen	⦶

Draw **one** line from each symbol to the correct compound.   [3 marks]

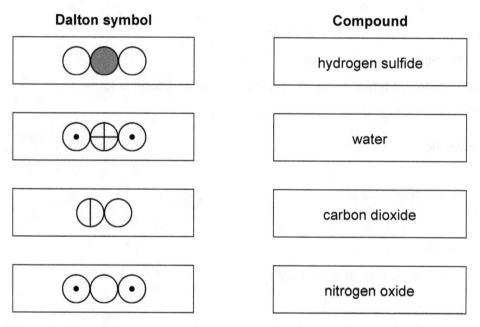

Dalton symbol   **Compound**

hydrogen sulfide

water

carbon dioxide

nitrogen oxide

4 The word equation shows the reaction between 2.4 g magnesium and 8.0 g copper oxide.

magnesium + copper oxide → magnesium oxide + copper

a. Describe what happens to the atoms during the reaction.   [2 marks]

_____

_____

b. During the reaction 4.0 g of magnesium oxide was produced.

Calculate the mass of copper. Show your working.   [2 marks]

_____

_____

_____

Total marks _____ /16

Chemistry – Dalton's atomic theory core

Chemistry – Dalton's atomic theory

1   The ancient Greeks believed that everything was made up of very tiny particles, called atoms, and that all atoms were the same.

In 1803 Dalton proposed a new theory in which he stated that not all atoms were the same but depended on the type of matter.

   a.   Suggest a reason why it took 2000 years for someone to come up with a new theory.   **[1 mark]**

_____

   b.   Identify **two** statements that **do not** fit with Dalton's atomic theory.   **[2 marks]**

      Tick **two** boxes.

      All matter is made of atoms.   ☐

      During a chemical reaction atoms are rearranged.   ☐

      Subatomic particles are found in the centre of an atom.   ☐

      Atoms of the same element are the same.   ☐

      Atoms of different elements are the same.   ☐

   c.   Complete the sentence.   **[1 mark]**

      When two or more different types of atoms join together a _____ is formed.

2   Dalton invented different symbols for atoms and molecules.

The diagrams below show different combinations of atoms.

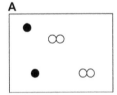 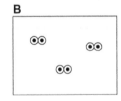 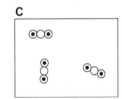 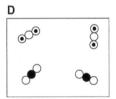

   a.   Write down the letter of the diagram which shows a **pure** element.   **[1 mark]**

      _____

   b.   Write down the letter of the diagram which shows a mixture of **two** compounds   **[1 mark]**

      _____

   c.   Write down the letter of a diagram which shows **two** different types of atoms.   **[1 mark]**

      _____

3 John Dalton did lots of experiments.

He developed a relative atomic weight scale, based on hydrogen having a mass of 1 unit.

He used this scale to work out the atomic weight of other elements.

When one atom of hydrogen combines with one atom of fluorine to form a molecule of hydrogen fluoride, the hydrogen to fluorine mass ratio is 1 : 19.

a. Calculate the relative atomic mass of fluorine. [1 mark]

_____

When 1 g of hydrogen reacts with 19 g of fluorine, 20 g of hydrogen fluoride is formed.

b. Use Dalton's atomic theory to explain why. [3 marks]

_____

_____

_____

_____

c. Calculate the mass of the water molecule. [1 mark]

1 oxygen atom   2 hydrogen atoms   1 water molecule

16 mass units   2 × 1 mass unit   _____

d. Use Dalton's atomic theory to explain your answer to part **c**. [2 marks]

_____

_____

e. Complete particle diagram.

Calculate the mass of carbon dioxide atoms. [2 marks]

12 g of carbon atoms   32 g of oxygen atoms   _____ of carbon dioxide atoms

Total marks _____ /16

Chemistry – Dalton's atomic theory extended

Physics – Movement: speed and acceleration

1 Choose the correct equation for average speed.

Tick **one** box. **[1 mark]**

$$\text{average speed} = \frac{\text{time taken}}{\text{distance travelled}} \quad \square$$

$$\text{average speed} = \frac{\text{distance travelled}}{\text{time taken}} \quad \square$$

$$\text{average speed} = \frac{\text{acceleration}}{\text{time taken}} \quad \square$$

$$\text{average speed} = \frac{\text{acceleration}}{\text{distance travelled}} \quad \square$$

2 Choose **two** units that measure the speed of an object.

Tick **two** boxes. **[2 marks]**

seconds per metre $\qquad \square$

kilometres per hour $\qquad \square$

kilometre-hours $\qquad \square$

metre-seconds $\qquad \square$

metres per second $\qquad \square$

3 The diagram shows a distance–time graph for a car.

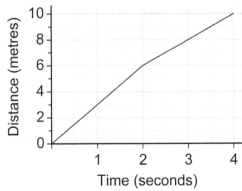

a. Calculate the average speed of the car in the first two seconds. You must state the units.
Show all your working out. **[2 marks]**

_____

_____

Answer _____ units _____

b. We know that at 2 seconds into the journey, a force was applied.
Use the graph to explain how we know this. **[1 mark]**

_____

4 The diagrams show three distance–time graphs.

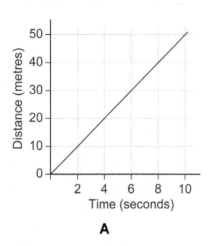 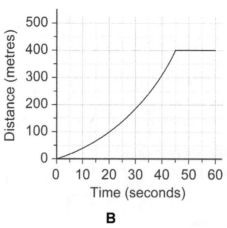 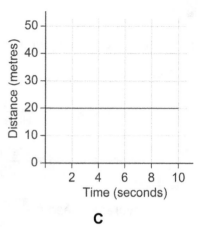

           A   **B**   **C**

Write **one** letter in each box.   **[3 marks]**

Identify which graph shows:

    a stationary object

    an object that accelerates then stops moving

    an object travelling at a constant speed.

5 The diagram shows distance–time graphs for three different trains, **A**, **B** and **C**.

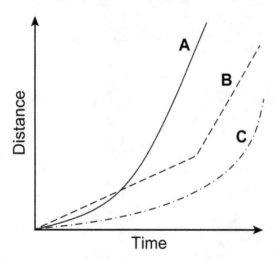

a. The three trains start at the same time.

    Identify which train starts more slowly than train **B** but then overtakes it.

    Write **one** letter in the box.   **[1 mark]**

b. A passenger train needs to travel fast, but it should accelerate gently to make the passengers feel comfortable.

    Choose the train that would be the best passenger train.

    Write **one** letter in the box.   **[1 mark]**

6 A student measures the time it takes a cyclist to travel 500 m in a race.

The student calculates that the cyclist travelled at 5 m/s.

The cyclist says that when they finished the race, the speedometer on their bicycle showed they were travelling at 8 m/s.

Explain the difference between the two speeds measured. **[2 marks]**

_____

_____

7 Train **A** passes through Yellow Station and Green Station at a constant speed without stopping.
Train **B** passes through Green Station and Yellow Station at a constant speed without stopping.

The two stations are 1.75 km apart.

The graph shows the journeys of two trains on a distance–time graph.

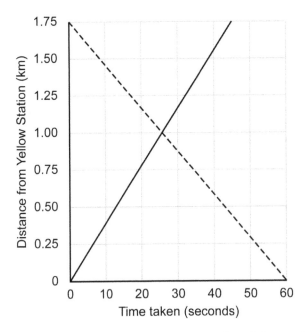

The solid line on the graph shows the distance travelled and time taken by train **A**.

The dashed line shows the distance travelled and time taken by train **B**.

a. Describe the journey of train **B**, relative to train **A**. **[2 marks]**

_____

_____

b. Estimate the distance from Yellow Station where train **A** and train **B** pass each other. **[1 mark]**

_____

Total marks _____ /16

Physics – Movement: speed and acceleration

1 Write down the equation for the average speed of an object. **[2 marks]**

   average speed = ─────────────────────────

2 A bus travels at a speed of 40 km/h between bus stops.
   The route it travels contains ten bus stops.

   a. Predict the average speed of the bus.

   Tick **one** box. **[1 mark]**

   The average speed of the bus will be:

   more than 40 km/h ☐

   equal to 40 km/h ☐

   less than 40 km/h ☐

   b. Justify your answer to part **a**. **[1 mark]**

   _____

   _____

3 The diagram shows a distance–time graph for a car.

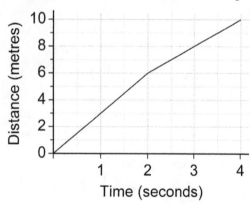

   a. Calculate the average speed of the car in the first two seconds.
   You **must** state the units. Show all your working. **[2 marks]**

   _____

   _____

   _____

   Answer _____ units_____

   b. We know that at 2 seconds into the journey, a force was applied.
   Use the graph to explain how we know this. **[1 mark]**

   _____

   _____

4 The diagrams show three distance–time graphs.

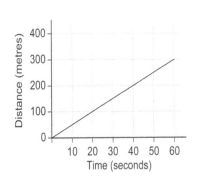

A

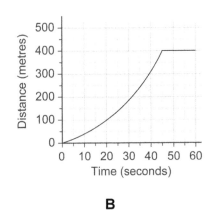

B

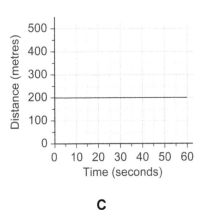

C

a. **i.** One of these graphs shows an object travelling at a constant speed.

Give the letter of this graph.　　　　　　　　　　　　　　　　　　　　**[1 mark]**

Graph ☐

ii. Calculate the average speed. You **must** show your working.　　　**[2 marks]**

_____

_____

_____

_____

Answer _____ m/s

b. **i.** One of these graphs shows an object that accelerates and then stops moving.

Give the letter of this graph.

Graph ☐　　　　　　　　　　　　　　　　　　　　　　　　　　**[1 mark]**

ii. Calculate the average speed over 60 seconds. You **must** show your working.　**[2 marks]**

_____

_____

_____

_____

Answer _____ m/s

5 Train **A** passes through Yellow Station to Green Station at a constant speed without stopping.

The two stations are 1.75 km apart.

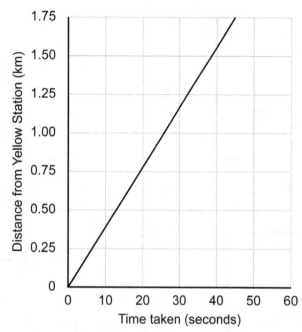

The line shows the distance travelled and time taken by train **A**.

a. Train **B** travels between Green Station to Yellow Station in one minute at a constant speed.

Sketch train **B**'s journey on the same graph as train **A**'s journey.   **[2 marks]**

b. Estimate the distance from Yellow Station where train **A** and train **B** pass each other.   **[1 mark]**

_____

Total marks _____ /16

Physics – Forces and gravity

1 Give the units for the following quantities.   **[3 marks]**

    mass   _____

    force   _____

    weight   _____

2 Complete the sentences.

   Choose from the list of terms and write **one** term in each gap.

   You do not need to use all the terms.   **[3 marks]**

       mass   **weight**   **contact**   **non-contact**   **force**

   A push or pull on an object is called a _____.

   Gravity acts between all objects that have _____.

   Gravity acts even between objects that are far apart. We say that gravity is a
   _____ force.

3 The diagram shows two planets, **A** and **B**.

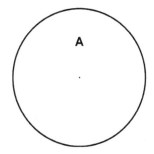 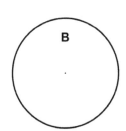

   a. Draw an arrow to show the direction of the gravitational force that acts on object **B** due
        to the masses of objects **A** and **B**. Label the force **F**.   **[1 mark]**

   On planet **A**, the gravitational field strength is 3.5 N/kg.

   The weight *W* of an object is given by the equation:

     $W = mg$

   where m = mass of object and g = gravitational field strength.

   b. Calculate the weight of a 20 kg object on planet **A**.   **[2 marks]**

   _____

   _____

   _____

   _____

4   The table compares the mass and weight of the same object on three different planets: Earth, Mercury and Jupiter.

Complete the blank statements in the table. Use the words 'less than', 'more than' or 'same as'.

(Remember: Mercury is smaller than Earth. Jupiter is much larger than Earth.)   **[3 marks]**

	Mass of object (kg)	**Weight of object (N)**
On Earth	10	100
On Mercury	_____ on Earth	_____ on Earth
On Jupiter	_____ on Earth	_____ on Earth

5   The graph shows the motion of a ball dropped from the top of a 125 m high tower. The ball comes to a standstill when it lands.

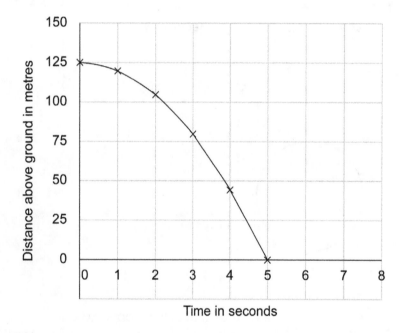

a.   Explain the shape of the graph. What does the changing gradient tell us?   **[2 marks]**

_____

_____

_____

_____

b.   Complete the graph by drawing a line to show what happens to the ball after 5 seconds.   **[2 marks]**

Total marks _____ /16

Physics – Forces and gravity

extended

1 Write down the equation that links weight, mass and gravitational field strength. [1 mark]

_____

2 The diagram shows two planets, **A** and **B**.

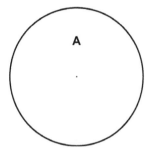 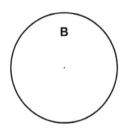

a. Draw an arrow to show the direction of the gravitational force that acts on object **B** due to the masses of objects **A** and **B**. Label the force **F**. [1 mark]

b. Describe the gravitational force that acts on object A due to the masses of objects **A** and **B**.
You should say something about the size and the direction of the force. [2 marks]

_____

_____

3 The table compares the mass and weight of the same object on three different planets:

Earth, Mercury and Jupiter.

a. Work out the missing values in the table. [3 marks]

	Gravitational field strength (N/kg)	Mass of object (kg)	Weight of object (N)
On Earth	10	10	100
On Mercury	3.7	_____	_____
On Jupiter	_____	_____	248

b. State how the mass of Jupiter compares to the mass of Earth. [1 mark]

_____

4 In an experiment, a ball with mass 0.20 kg is dropped, in a vacuum, from the top of a 125 m high tower. The ball does not bounce when it reaches the ground.

The graph shows the motion of the ball.

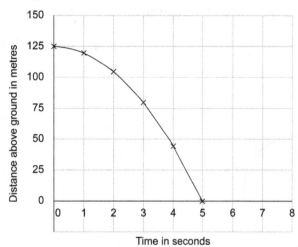

a. State what quantity can be worked out by calculating the gradient at a point on the graph. [1 mark]

_____

b. Explain why the graph is not a straight line. [1 mark]

_____

_____

c. The experiment is repeated with a ball that is exactly the same shape but has a mass of 0.50 kg.

Compare the graph that would be obtained with the graph for the mass of 0.20 kg.

Justify your answer. [2 marks]

_____

_____

5 The gravitational field strength on the surface of Earth is approximately 10 N/kg.
Space probes that investigate the solar system travel long distances away from Earth.

a. Describe how the gravitational field strength of Earth changes as a space probe travels further away. [2 marks]

_____

_____

b. Pluto is a dwarf planet. It has a mass that is approximately $\frac{1}{500}$ times that of Earth.

Suggest how the gravitational field strength of Pluto is different to that of Earth.

Give a reason for your answer. [2 marks]

_____

_____

Total marks _____ /16

Physics – Forces and gravity extended

Physics – Electric circuits: current, potential difference and resistance

1 Match each description to the electrical quantity from the list.

Write the quantity in the answer box.   **[3 marks]**

potential difference   current   resistance

Description	Quantity
Opposition to the flow of charge, measured in ohms, Ω	_____
The flow of charge, measured in amperes, A	_____
The amount of energy transferred from a battery to the movement of charge, measured in volts, V	_____

2 Match the electrical component symbols to the names of the components.

Draw **one** line from each symbol to the component name.   **[4 marks]**

Symbol	Component name

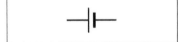

resistor

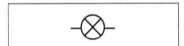

cell

lamp

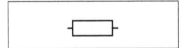

ammeter

3 A student sets up an electrical circuit to test different components.
This is their description of the circuit:

'All the components are connected one after the other. The potential difference is shared between the components.'

a. Choose whether the circuit is a series or parallel circuit.

Tick **one** box. [1 mark]

Series ☐

Parallel ☐

b. Write a description of the other type of circuit. [2 marks]

_____

_____

4 The diagram shows a circuit in a new design of torch. The lamp is a filament bulb that has a high resistance and produces a lot of heat.

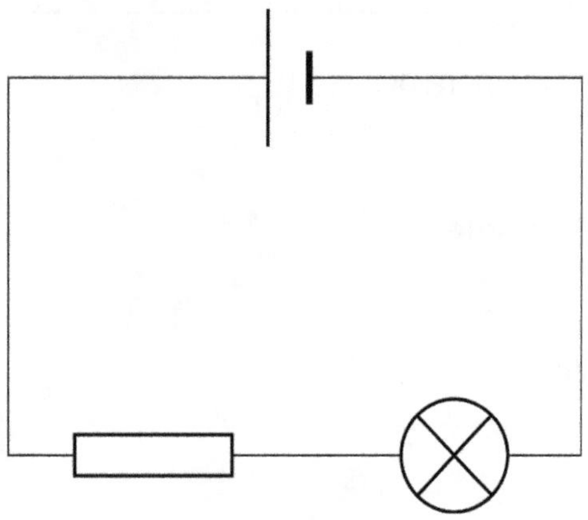

a. Name the component that could be added to control whether the lamp is on or off. [1 mark]

_____

b. The torch is tested and it does not shine brightly enough.

Suggest **two** ways that the circuit could be changed to make the torch shine more brightly. [2 marks]

1 _____

2 _____

5 The diagram shows a parallel circuit. Each branch contains a resistor with a resistance of 100 Ω.

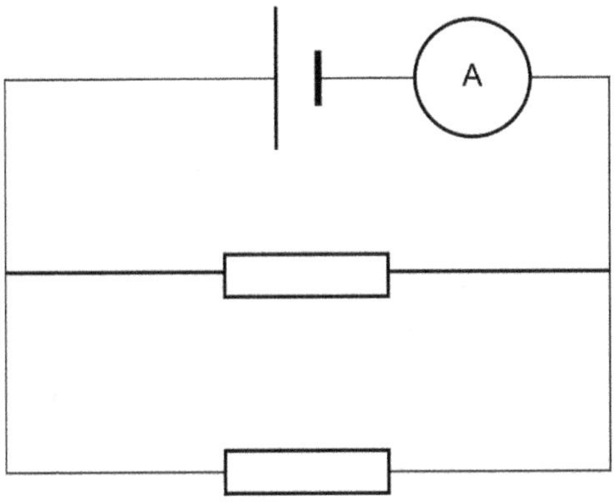

a. The ammeter next to the cell measures a current of 30 mA.

Choose the correct value for the current in each resistor. [1 mark]

7.5 mA ☐

15 mA ☐

30 mA ☐

60 mA ☐

b. Draw another circuit diagram to show the two resistors connected in series.

Include the ammeter in your diagram. [1 mark]

c. The ammeter in this new circuit measures a current of 7.5 mA.

Choose the correct value of the current in each resistor.

Tick **one** box. [1 mark]

7.5 mA ☐

15 mA ☐

30 mA ☐

60 mA ☐

Total marks _____ /16

Physics – Electric circuits: current, potential difference and resistance core

Physics – Electric circuits: current, potential difference and resistance

1 Name the components shown.

a. _____ **[1 mark]**

b. —(V)— _____ **[1 mark]**

c. _____ **[1 mark]**

d. —|⊢ _____ **[1 mark]**

2 A student sets up an electrical circuit to test different components.

This is their description of the circuit:

> 'All the components are connected one after the other. The potential difference is shared between the components.'

a. Choose whether the circuit is a series or parallel circuit.

Tick **one** box. **[1 mark]**

Series ☐

Parallel ☐

b. Write a description of the other type of circuit. **[2 marks]**

_____

_____

3 The diagrams show the two different ways of connecting two lamps in a circuit with a battery.

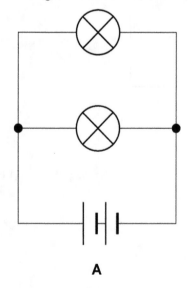

A

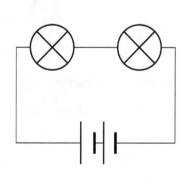

B

a. The lamps shine more brightly in circuit **A** than in circuit **B**. Explain why this happens. **[2 marks]**

_____

_____

_____

b. If both circuits are made and left switched on, the battery lasts twice as long in circuit **B**.

Suggest why this happens. **[2 marks]**

_____

_____

_____

4 The table shows the resistance of different circuit components.

Use the data in the table to answer the questions.

Component	Resistance (Ω)
copper wire	0.000 001
variable resistor	0 to 1000
PVC plastic	1 000 000

a. Choose the best component to use as an insulator. **[1 mark]**

_____

b. In a cinema, the lights need to be bright before the film so that people can see where they are going. Once the film starts, the lights need to be made very dim.

Choose the component needed for a cinema lights circuit. Explain your answer. **[2 marks]**

_____

_____

c. Explain why the cables used to connect home appliances to the mains electricity supply are usually made from copper coated in PVC plastic. **[2 marks]**

_____

_____

Total marks _____ /16

Physics – Static electricity

1 Choose whether these are contact forces or non-contact forces.

Write 'contact' or 'non-contact' alongside each force. **[3 marks]**

Gravity _____

Person pushing on a shopping trolley _____

Static electricity _____

2 When a person combs their hair, they notice that some hairs appear to 'float' in the air.

Complete these sentences to explain what is happening. Choose from the words in the list. You do not need to use all the words in the list. **[5 marks]**

> **gravity   protons   friction   positively   electrons**
>
> **repel   negatively   attract**

The surface of the hair and the comb rub together. This produces a force of _____ .

This force causes _____ to transfer from the hair to the comb.

The hair becomes _____ charged and the comb becomes _____ charged.

The opposite charges _____ so the hair moves towards the comb.

3 The diagram shows three balls suspended on cotton thread.

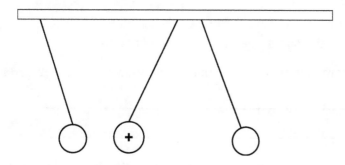

The middle ball is positively charged. The other balls are attracted or repelled by the middle ball.

Write the sign of the electric charge on each ball. **[2 marks]**

4 The diagram shows an experiment that uses a Van de Graaff generator.

Inside the large metal globe is a belt made of insulating material.

A motor drives this belt, so it rubs against the inside surface of the metal globe.

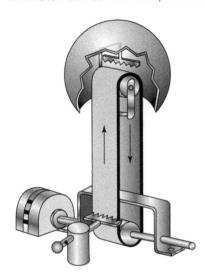

   a. Describe how electrical charge can be made to build up on the
       Van de Graaff generator.   **[2 marks]**

   _____

   _____

   b. Suggest **one** suitable safety precaution a student could take before using
       the apparatus.   **[1 mark]**

   _____

5 Thunderstorms cause electrical charges to build up on clouds and tall buildings.

Explain why tall buildings often have metal rods or wires running from the tallest
part of the building to the ground.   **[3 marks]**

_____

_____

_____

_____

_____

_____

Total marks _____ **/16**

Physics – Static electricity

1 An electrical charge has an electrical field surrounding it. This field produces non-contact forces when other electrical charges are present.

   a. Give the meaning of the expression 'non-contact force'.   **[1 mark]**

   _____

   b. Name the common particles that have a negative electrical charge.   **[1 mark]**

   _____

2 An insulator rubbed with a cloth can build up electrical charge, as shown in the diagram.

   Rods made from different materials behave differently: some become negatively charged when rubbed, others become positively charged.

   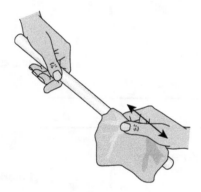

   A student designs an experiment to test whether different rubbed rods attract or repel each other.

   a. Give the name of the independent variable in this experiment.   **[1 mark]**

   _____

   b. Use your knowledge of static electricity to complete the table of results. **[3 marks]**

	Rod 1	
Rod 2	Plastic (polythene)	Perspex
Plastic (polythene)	_____	Attract
Perspex	_____	_____

3 The diagram shows an experiment that uses a Van de Graaff generator.

Inside the large metal globe is a belt made of insulating material.

A motor drives this belt, so it rubs against the inside surface of the metal globe.

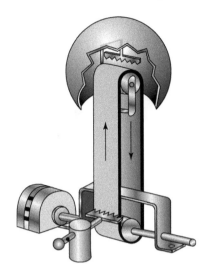

a. Describe how electrical charge can be made to build up on the
   Van de Graaff generator.   [2 marks]

   _____

   _____

b. Suggest **one** suitable safety precaution a student could take before
   using the apparatus.   [1 mark]

   _____

4 Explain why wet weather can affect the results of static electricity experiments.   [3 marks]

   _____

   _____

5 The diagram shows a gold-leaf electroscope. This can be used to detect electrical charge.

The gold leaf is very thin and light, so only a small force is needed to lift it up.

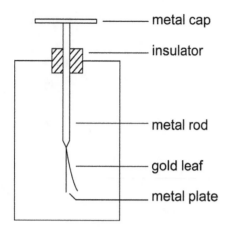

metal cap

insulator

metal rod

gold leaf

metal plate

a. An electrically charged object is brought close to the top of the electroscope.
The gold leaf lifts upwards.

Suggest an explanation for this observation. **[2 marks]**

_____

_____

b. A student touches the top of the electroscope and the foil drops down to its normal position.
Explain what has happened. **[2 marks]**

_____

_____

_____

_____

Total marks _____ /16

Physics – Energy: stores, transfers, power and costs

`core`

1 Draw **one** line from each energy store to the correct description. **[3 marks]**

Energy store	Description
chemical energy store	a stretched spring
thermal energy store	gas that is burned to heat a saucepan
elastic energy store	a saucepan full of hot water

2 The diagram shows the first part of an electricity bill for a family home.

Use the information in the bill to answer the questions.

Meter readings				
			(E = estimate, C = customer, A = actual)	
Period	**Meter number**	**Start reading/kW h**	**End reading/kW h**	**Reader**
1 Mar to 31 Mar	S088 06654	12 549	12 675	C
1 Apr to 31 Apr	S088 06654	12 675	12 807	A

a. Write out the full name of the unit shown by 'kW h'. **[1 mark]**

_____

b. Complete the missing terms in the table. **[2 marks]**

Month	Final meter reading (kWh)	Initial meter reading (kWh)	Amount of energy used (kWh)
March			
April			

c.   Electricity costs 5.7p per kW h. Calculate the total cost of electricity used between 1 March and 30 April. You **must** show your working.   [2 marks]

_____

_____

3   The diagram shows an electric circuit containing three cells and three lamps.

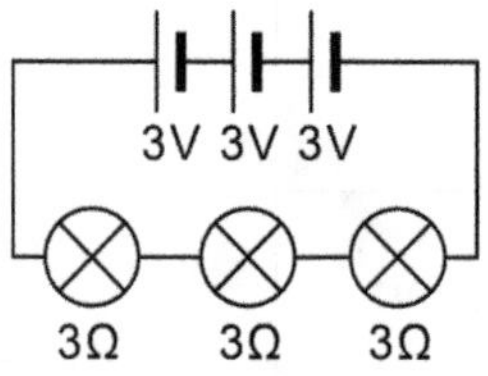

a.   Complete the diagram of the energy transfer that takes place inside each **cell**.   [1 mark]

| chemical energy store | → | _____ energy store |

b.   An energy transfer takes place within each lamp, which increases the thermal energy store of the lamp and surroundings.

Name **two** processes involved in this energy transfer.   [2 marks]

1 _____

2 _____

c.   The circuit components and surroundings store energy before the circuit is connected up.

They also store energy after the circuit is connected up.

Identify the correct statement about the total amount of energy stored in the circuit components and the surroundings.

Tick **one** box.   [1 mark]

Total energy stored is higher **after** the circuit is connected up.   ☐

Total energy stored is higher **before** the circuit is connected up.   ☐

Total energy stored stays the same.   ☐

4   The table shows some nutritional information for different types of food. All the values show what is obtained in a 100 g serving of the food.

Food	Protein (g)	Fat (g)	Carbohydrates (g)	Of which sugars (g)	Energy (kJ)
white bread	7.7	1.5	45.5	3.8	985
chicken fillets	23.9	6.7	0.2	0.0	157
milk chocolate	7.3	30.0	57.0	56.0	2232

a. Name the food that gives the highest amount of energy per 100 g.   **[1 mark]**

_____

b. Not all the energy we get from the food we eat is transferred to useful activities such as running or walking.

Suggest **one** energy transfer that wastes the energy we get from food.   **[1 mark]**

_____

5   A student builds a model crane. She includes an electrical circuit to power a motor to lift objects.

The table shows her predictions for the amount of energy transferred at each stage.

Stage 1	Stage 2		Stage 3		Stage 4
Chemical energy of battery (J)	Electrical energy transferred by motor (J)	Increase in thermal store (J)	Kinetic energy of moving object + work done on object (J)	Increase in thermal store (J)	Change in potential energy of lifted object (J)
15	12	3	7	5	9

One of the values in the bottom row of the table is wrong. Identify which value must be wrong.

Explain your answer.   **[2 marks]**

_____

_____

Total marks _____ /16

Physics – Energy: stores, transfers, power and costs

1   The diagram shows a tennis ball falling towards the floor. The ball is released from position **A**.

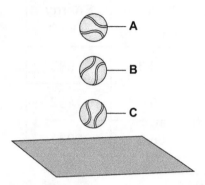

Complete the following sentences. Use words from the list. You do not need to use all the words from the list   **[4 marks]**

| |
| kinetic   potential   total   transfers   elastic   thermal |

The gravitational _____ energy is at a maximum at point A.

As the ball falls, energy _____ from this store to a different store.

This different energy store is due to the movement of the ball.
It is a _____ energy store.

Conservation of energy tells us that the _____ energy stored stays constant.

2   The diagram shows a Sankey diagram for an energy-efficient electric light bulb.

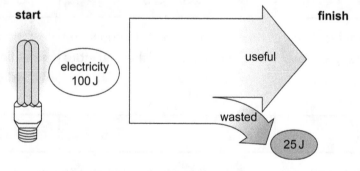

a.   Describe how a Sankey diagram shows the principle of conservation of energy.   **[1 mark]**

_____

b.   Calculate the useful energy.   **[1 mark]**

_____

c.   Describe the energy transfer that accounts for most of the wasted energy.   **[1 mark]**

_____

3 The diagram shows a spring in three different positions.

In position **A**, the spring hangs by itself. In positions **B** and **C**, weights have been added to stretch the spring.

A   B   C

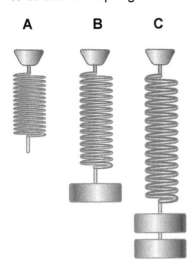

a.   Identify the position when the spring has the largest store of **elastic potential** energy.

   Tick **one** box.   [1 mark]

   Position **A**   ☐

   Position **B**   ☐

   Position **C**   ☐

   All diagrams show the same amount.   ☐

b.   The weight in position **C** is carefully taken off the spring and the spring is let go.
   The elastic energy is transferred to other energy stores.

   Describe **two** of these energy transfers.   [2 marks]

   1 _____

   2 _____

Physics – Energy: stores, transfers, power and costs extended

4 A team of students set up an experiment to compare the energy available from different kinds of food. They measured the temperature change when the food is burnt to estimate the amount of energy given out.

The diagram shows the apparatus they used.

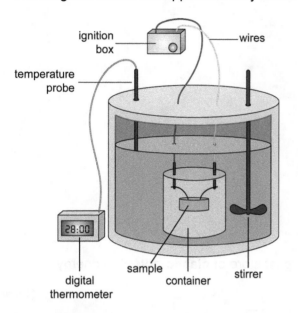

The table shows their measurements.

Food	Energy per 100 g (kJ)
white bread	985
chicken fillets	157
milk chocolate	2232

a. The students wrote some conclusions for their investigation.

Decide whether each conclusion is true, false or you cannot tell.

Tick **one** box for each conclusion.   **[3 marks]**

Conclusion	True	False	Cannot tell
Milk chocolate stored the most energy per 100 g.	☐	☐	☐
A diet containing only milk chocolate is best.	☐	☐	☐
The foods cannot be compared because the portion sizes were different.	☐	☐	☐

b. Suggest how thermal insulating material could be used to improve the experiment.   **[1 mark]**

_____

_____

5 The table compares the costs of different ways to generate electricity.

Type of power station	Cost in pence per kW h
gas	8.0
coal	10.2
nuclear	8.1
onshore wind farm	9.5
solar	16.9

Suggest **two** reasons why the total electricity demand for the UK is **not** provided by gas-fuelled power stations. **[2 marks]**

1 _____

2 _____

Total marks _____ /16

Physics – The Earth in space

1   Choose the correct order. Start with the smallest and finish with the largest.

Tick **one** box.   [1 mark]

star	planet	galaxy	Universe	☐
galaxy	star	Universe	planet	☐
planet	star	galaxy	Universe	☐
Universe	galaxy	star	planet	☐

2   Look at the diagram of the Earth.

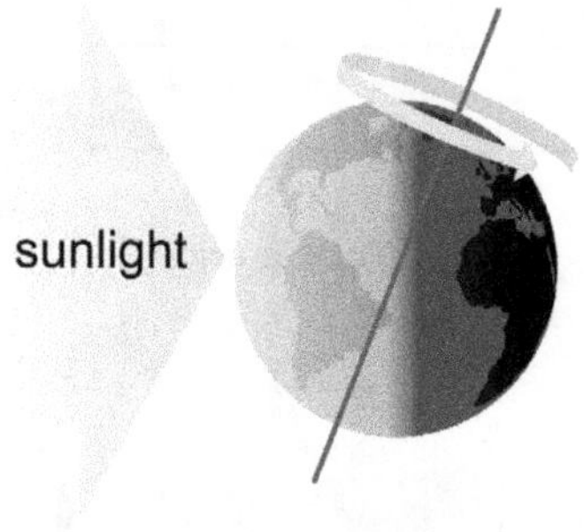

sunlight

a.   In each 24-hour period we have day and night.

Explain why.   [1 mark]

_____

_____

b.   When it is daytime in South America, it is night-time in Great Britain.

Explain why.   [1 mark]

_____

_____

Look at the diagram showing how the Earth moves around the Sun.

23°

– northern hemisphere is
tilted towards the Sun

– northern hemisphere is
tilted away from the Sun

c.   Label the diagram.

Choose from these words.   [2 marks]

summer in the UK   autumn in the UK   winter in the UK   spring in the UK

d.   Complete the following sentences.

Choose from these words.   [3 marks]

away from   towards   southern   northern   winter   spring

It is summer in the UK when the _____ hemisphere is

tilted _____ the Sun.

At the same time it will be _____ in the southern hemisphere.

e.   At mid-winter, 21 December, how much daylight would you expect to see at the North Pole?

Circle **one** number.   [1 mark]

0 hours   6 hours   12 hours   18 hours   24 hours

3 Models of our Universe have changed over time. 2000 years ago a Greek philosopher called Ptolemy believed that the Universe was arranged in layers.

The diagram shows Ptolemy's model of the Universe.

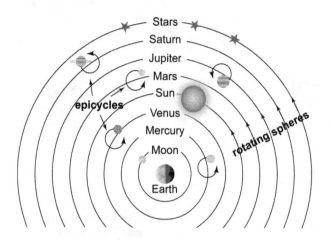

a. Describe Ptolemy's model of the Universe. **[2 marks]**

_____

_____

About 500 years ago, the Polish astronomer Copernicus came up with a new theory. He suggested that the Sun was at the centre of the system. The Earth and other planets orbited the Sun.

b. Suggest a reason why Copernicus' theory was not widely accepted. **[1 mark]**

_____

_____

About 400 years ago the Italian astronomer Galileo collected evidence with his new telescope which supported Copernicus' theory. However, the Catholic Church did not accept the new theory.

c. Describe how Galileo collected his evidence. **[1 mark]**

_____

_____

d. Suggest a reason why the Catholic Church did not accept Galileo's theory. **[1 mark]**

_____

_____

e. Eventually Galileo's theory was accepted.

Explain why. **[2 marks]**

_____

_____

Total marks _____ /16

Physics – The Earth in space core

Physics – The Earth in space

1 Look at the this graph.

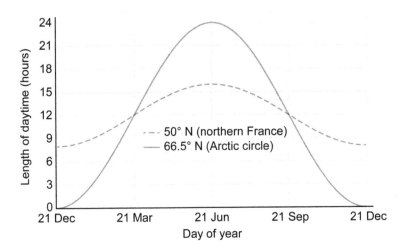

a. Compare the length of a summer's day in the Arctic Circle with that in northern France. **[1 mark]**

_____

_____

b. Explain why the length of daytime varies throughout the year. **[2 marks]**

_____

_____

2 The table shows some approximate distances in the Universe.

Examples in the Universe	Distance (ly)
Distance across the Milky Way galaxy	100 000
Earth to Sirius (one of our closest stars)	8.6
Earth to the most distant point of the Universe	15 000 000 000
Earth to Pluto (at their closest)	0.000 44
Earth to the Sun	0.000 016
Earth to the Andromeda galaxy	2 500 000

a. Write down what the unit **ly** means **[1 mark]**

_____

b. Suggest a reason why distances across the Universe are not measured in kilometres. **[1 mark]**

_____

_____

c. Compare the distance between Pluto and the Sun and the distance between the Earth and the Sun when Pluto is at its closest point to the Earth.

[1 mark]

_____

_____

d. A student is star gazing. It is a clear night. Our nearest star is Sirius. It is in clear view.

A little later the student observes stars in the Milky Way.

Explain why he is not seeing Sirius and the stars in the Milky Way at the same point in time.

[3 marks]

_____

_____

_____

_____

3 The diagram shows the phases of the Moon.

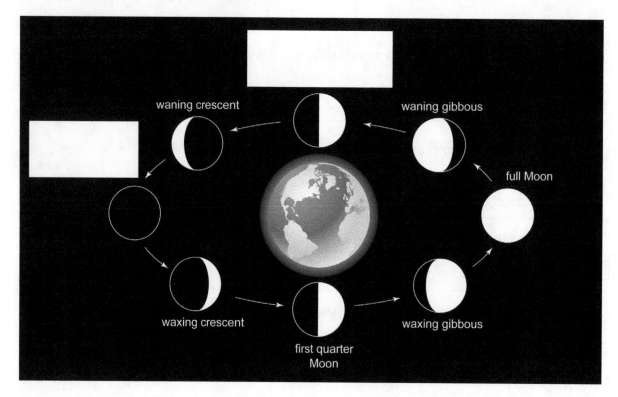

a. Complete the diagram. [1 mark]

b. Explain why different phases of the Moon are observed each month. [2 marks]

_____

_____

_____

_____

c. The planet Venus does not produce its own light but is clearly visible from the night sky at certain times of the year.

Explain why. [1 mark]

_____

_____

4 Models of our Universe have changed over time. Here are some of the early ideas.

- 2000 years ago a Greek philosopher called Ptolemy believed that the Universe was arranged in layers, with the Earth in the middle and the stars at the outer edge.

- 500 years ago, Copernicus came up with a new theory. He suggested that the Sun was at the centre of the system. The Earth and other planets orbited the Sun.

- 400 years later Galileo collected evidence with his new telescope which supported Copernicus' theory. However, the Catholic Church did not accept the new theory.

Explain why it took such a long time for Copernicus' theory to be accepted. [3 marks]

_____

_____

_____

_____

_____

Total marks _____ /16

Biology – Breathing and gas exchange

1   The diagram shows parts of the respiratory system for gas exchange in human breathing.

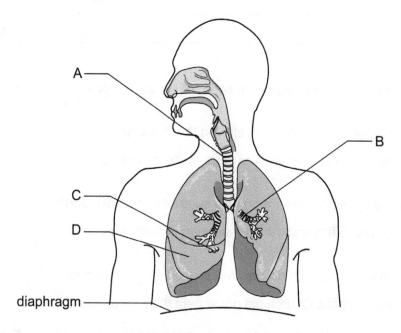

   a.   State the letter showing the trachea.   **[1 mark]**

   _____

   b.   State the letter showing a bronchus.   **[1 mark]**

   _____

2   Complete the following sentences. Choose from these words.   **[2 marks]**

   decreases   **increases**   **inwards**   **outwards**

   When we inhale, muscles between the ribs contract and move the ribcage upwards and
   _____. Muscles in the diaphragm contract to flatten it. This _____the
   volume of the chest cavity.

3   Gas exchange takes place in the alveoli when a person breathes. The diagram shows an alveolus
   in the lung.

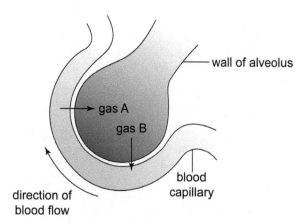

a. Give the name of gas **A**.   [1 mark]

_____

b. Give the name of gas **B**.   [1 mark]

_____

c. Which of the following features makes the alveoli well adapted for gas exchange?

Tick **two** boxes.   [2 marks]

Dry walls ☐

A large surface area ☐

Thick walls ☐

A good blood supply ☐

d. Cigarette smoke damages the walls of the alveoli. The alveoli walls break down, forming larger air spaces than normal.

Explain how this affects gas exchange in the lungs.   [2 marks]

_____

_____

4 The diagram shows a model of the lungs.

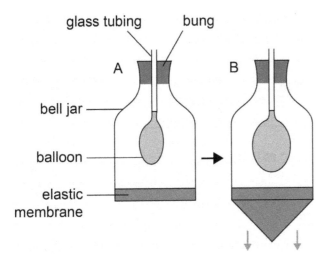

a. State what is represented by the balloon.   [1 mark]

_____

b. State what is represented by the elastic membrane.   [1 mark]

_____

c.   Diagram **B** shows the elastic membrane being pulled downwards. This causes the balloon to get bigger.

Explain why.   [2 marks]

_____

_____

5   Some scientists collected data to investigate the link between height and lung volume. They measured the height and lung volume of a group of men. The results are shown in the graph.

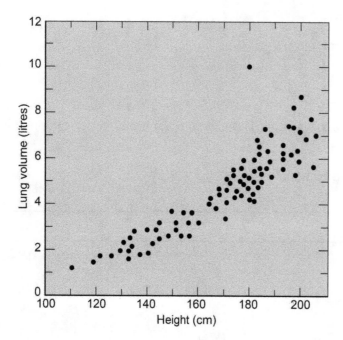

a.   Describe the pattern shown by the data.   [1 mark]

_____

b.   One man in the investigation was an Olympic athlete.

How tall was this man?   [1 mark]

_____ cm

Total marks _____ /16

Biology – Breathing and gas exchange

1   The diagram shows parts of the respiratory system for gas exchange in humans.

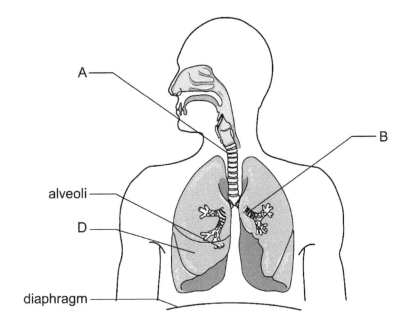

Name the parts labelled **A** and **B**.

A _____   [1 mark]

B _____   [1 mark]

2   The diagram shows gas exchange in an alveolus.

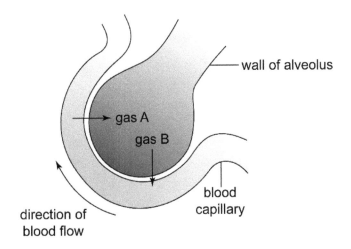

a.   Give the name of gas **A**.   [1 mark]

_____

b.   Give the name of gas **B**.   [1 mark]

_____

c. Explain how gas exchange happens in the alveoli. [2 marks]

_____

_____

d. The alveoli are surrounded by blood vessels called capillaries. Capillary walls are only one cell thick.

Explain how this feature of capillaries helps gas exchange. [1 mark]

_____

_____

e. Cigarette smoke damages the walls of the alveoli. The alveoli walls break down, forming larger air spaces than normal.

Explain how this affects gas exchange in the lungs. [2 marks]

_____

_____

3 Some scientists collected data to investigate the link between height and lung volume. They measured the height and lung volume of a group of men. The results are shown in the graph.

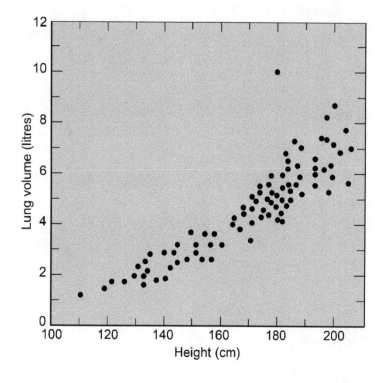

a. Describe what this data shows about the correlation between height and lung volume. [1 mark]

_____

b. One man in the investigation was an Olympic athlete. How tall was this man? [1 mark]

_____ cm

4 The diagram shows a model of the lungs.

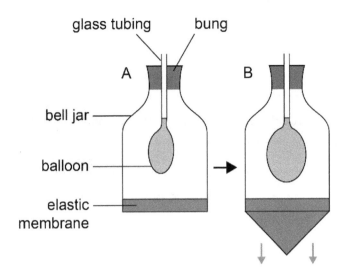

a. In this model, the balloon represents the lungs. State the name of the structure represented by the elastic membrane. **[1 mark]**

_____

b. Explain why the balloon expands when the elastic membrane is pulled down. **[2 marks]**

_____

_____

c. Predict what would happen if the elastic membrane is pushed upwards.

Explain your prediction. **[2 marks]**

_____

_____

Total marks _____ /16

Biology – Breathing and gas exchange extended

Biology – Digestion

1 Draw **one** line from each food group to the correct use in the body. **[2 marks]**

Food group	Use in the body
carbohydrates	provide reserve energy supply and insulation
proteins	provide energy
fats	important for growth and repair

2 The diagram shows the human digestive system.

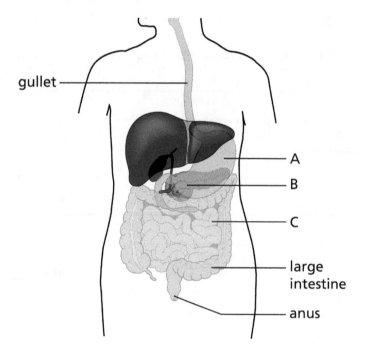

a. Write the letter that shows the small intestines. **[1 mark]**

_____

b. Write the letter that shows the stomach. **[1 mark]**

_____

c. Choose the statements that correctly describe how the stomach is adapted for its function.

Tick **two** boxes [2 marks]

Its walls have villi to give it a large surface area. ☐

It secretes acid to kill bacteria. ☐

It contains an enzyme to break down protein. ☐

It contains cilia to move food along. ☐

d. Describe what happens to food in the small intestines. [2 marks]

_____

_____

e. Name the part of the digestive system where water is reabsorbed into the blood. [1 mark]

_____

3 A person has been diagnosed with an iron deficiency. Which of the following foods should the person increase in their diet?

Tick **one** box. [1 mark]

Red meat, beans, pulses and green vegetables ☐

Citrus fruit and potatoes ☐

White meat and pasta ☐

Butter and cream ☐

4 The table shows the energy content of some different food and drink from a fast food chain.

Food	Energy (kJ)
1 large portion of chips	1900
1 cheeseburger	2280
cola	700
tomato ketchup	120

A woman went to a fast food restaurant for lunch. The woman ate a large portion of chips, a cheeseburger and a portion of tomato ketchup, and had a cola to drink.

a. Calculate the total amount of energy provided by the lunch, including the drink. **[1 mark]**

_____ kJ

b. An average woman needs about 8300 kJ per day.

Approximately what percentage of the daily energy requirement is provided by the woman's lunch?

Circle the correct value. **[1 mark]**

10%   **40%**   **60%**   **80%**

c. The woman eats fast food at least once a day.

Suggest why she is at risk of becoming obese. **[2 marks]**

_____

_____

5 The digestive system produces biological catalysts called digestive enzymes.

Explain the function of digestive enzymes. **[2 marks]**

_____

_____

Total marks _____ /16

Biology – Digestion

1   The diagram shows the human digestive system.

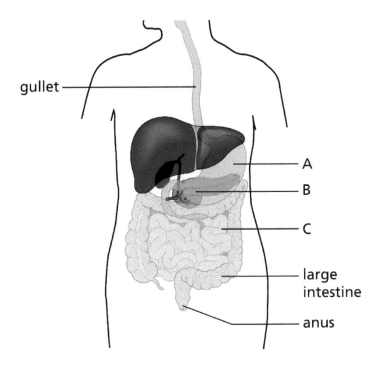

gullet

A

B

C

large intestine

anus

a. Name the organs **A** and **B**.   **[2 marks]**

A _____

B _____

b. Describe what happens to proteins in the small intestines.   **[2 marks]**

_____

_____

c. Describe why proteins are an important part of a balanced diet.   **[1 mark]**

_____

2   The diagram below shows villi which are found on the wall of the small intestine.

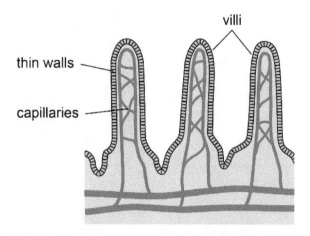

Explain how each feature of the small intestine is adapted to its function. The first row has been done for you as an example.   **[2 marks]**

Adaptation	Explanation
thin walls only one cell thick	allows molecules to diffuse easily from inside the intestine into blood
good blood supply	
finger-like shape of villi	

3   Celiac disease is a condition that causes damage to the villi in the small intestine. Damage to villi can lead to weight loss.

Suggest why.   **[1 marks]**

_____

4   A student has been diagnosed with anaemia, a nutritional deficiency.

The student's doctor has advised him to eat more nuts, green vegetables and red meat.

Explain why.   **[2 marks]**

_____

_____

5 The table shows the energy content of some different food and drink from a fast food chain.

Food	Energy (kJ)
1 large portion of chips	1900
1 cheeseburger	2280
cola	700
tomato ketchup	120

A woman went to a fast food restaurant for lunch. The woman ate a large portion of chips, a cheeseburger and a portion of tomato ketchup, and had a cola to drink.

a. Calculate the total amount of energy provided by the lunch, including the drink.　　　　**[1 mark]**

_____ kJ

b. An average woman needs about 8300 kJ per day.

Calculate what percentage of the woman's daily energy requirement is provided by her lunch.

[1 mark]

_____ %

c. The woman eats fast food at least once a day.

Explain why she is at risk of becoming obese.　　　　**[2 marks]**

_____

_____

d. A diet consisting only of fast food is likely to lead to malnutrition.

Explain why.　　　　**[2 marks]**

_____

_____

Total marks _____ /16

Biology – Respiration

1   Complete the following sentences. Choose from these words. **[2 marks]**

   chemical   **energy**   **glucose**   **physical**   **oxygen**

   Respiration is a _____ reaction that takes place in the cells of plants and
   animals. Respiration releases _____ which is needed for many life processes.

2   Oxygen and glucose are needed for aerobic respiration.

   a.   Complete the word equation for aerobic respiration.   **[1 mark]**

   glucose + oxygen → water + _____

   b.   In the human body, where does glucose for respiration come from?   **[1 mark]**

   _____

   c.   In the human body, where does oxygen for respiration come from?   **[1 mark]**

   _____

3   Where does aerobic respiration take place?

   Tick **one** box.   **[1 mark]**

   Only in the muscles   ☐

   Only in the lungs   ☐

   Only in the heart   ☐

   In all cells   ☐

4 Some students set up the apparatus shown below to investigate the effect of temperature on fermentation.

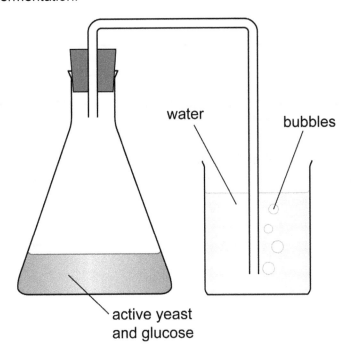

water

bubbles

active yeast
and glucose

In the conical flask they mixed active yeast with warm water and glucose. As the mixture fermented bubbles were produced.

The students counted the number of bubbles produced at different temperatures. The results are shown in the table below.

Temperature (°C)	10	20	30	40
Number of bubbles counted in one minute	4	10	23	52

a. Name the **independent** variable in the investigation. [1 mark]

_____

b. Name **one** variable that the students would need to keep the same. [1 mark]

_____

c. Explain why glucose was added to the yeast and warm water. [1 mark]

_____

d. Name the gas that formed the bubbles. [1 mark]

_____

e. Use the data in the table to draw a conclusion. [1 mark]

_____

5 Long distance runners often drink liquids that contain glucose.

Explain how this helps them perform well. **[2 marks]**

_____

_____

6 Athletes that run sprint distances cannot take in oxygen fast enough to meet the demands of the muscles.

    a. Complete the word equation to show the reactant and product for anaerobic respiration in a sprint athlete in the later stages of a race. **[1 mark]**

        glucose →_____

    b. Explain why anaerobic respiration takes place in sprint events such as a 100 m running race, but not during a gentle jog. **[2 marks]**

    _____

    _____

Total marks _____ /16

Biology – Respiration

1 Complete the following sentences. Choose from these words.   **[2 marks]**

        cells   **chemical**   **displacement**   **muscles**   **physical**

    Respiration is a _____ reaction that takes place in the _____
    of plants and animals.

2 What is the purpose of respiration?

    Tick **one** box.   **[1 mark]**

    To make oxygen   ☐

    To make glucose   ☐

    To release energy   ☐

    To make water   ☐

3 Respiration that uses oxygen as a reactant is known as aerobic respiration.

    a. Complete the word equation for aerobic respiration.   **[1 mark]**

          glucose + oxygen → water + _____

    b. Glucose is also a reactant in aerobic respiration.

          In the human body, where does the glucose come from?   **[1 mark]**

          _____

    c. Energy is not written as a product of respiration in a word equation.

          Explain why.   **[1 mark]**

          _____

4 Some students set up the apparatus shown below to investigate the effect of temperature on fermentation.

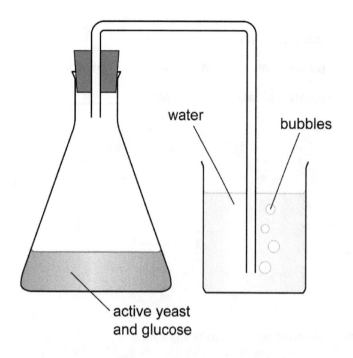

water   bubbles

active yeast
and glucose

In the conical flask they mixed active yeast with warm water and glucose.

As the mixture fermented bubbles were produced.

The students counted the number of bubbles that were produced at different temperatures.

a. Name **one** variable that the students would need to keep the same. [1 mark]

_____

b. Explain why glucose was added to the yeast and warm water. [1 mark]

_____

c. Complete the equation for the fermentation reaction that took place in the investigation.

[2 marks]

glucose → _____ + _____

5 An athlete competes in the 100 m hurdle event. At the end of the race the athlete continues to breathe at a faster rate and more deeply for several more minutes.

Explain why. [2 marks]

_____

_____

_____

6 Some students set up an investigation as shown in the diagram.

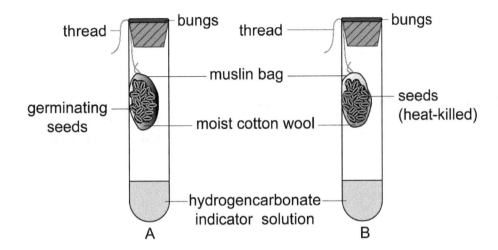

They left the apparatus for 2 hours and then checked for any colour changes in the indicator solution.

Hydrogen carbonate indicator turns from red to yellow in the presence of carbon dioxide.

The table shows their results.

Test tube	Colour of indicator solution after 2 hours
A	yellow
B	red

Explain why test tube **A** turned yellow but test tube **B** remained red. **[4 marks]**

_____

_____

_____

_____

Total marks _____ /16

Biology – Photosynthesis

1 Complete the following sentences.

Choose from these words. **[2 marks]**

chloroplasts   **glucose**   **heat**   **light**   **protein**

Plants use energy carried by _____ from the Sun. They use this energy to make

_____.

2 Why don't plants need to eat other plants or animals?

Tick **one** box. **[1 mark]**

Plants are not living organisms. ☐

Plants get everything they need from the soil. ☐

Plants can make their own food. ☐

Plants do not need any nutrients. ☐

3 Complete the word equation for photosynthesis using the following terms. **[2 marks]**

carbon dioxide   **ethanol**   **heat**   **minerals**   **oxygen**   **soil**

_____ + water → glucose + _____

4 Plants store some of the glucose they make as starch, so it can be used when needed.

Give **one** other way in which a plant uses the glucose it makes in photosynthesis. **[1 mark]**

_____

5 Draw **one** line from each adaptation of a leaf to the correct function. **[2 marks]**

Adaptation of leaf	**Function**
palisade cells are packed with chloroplasts	to control the movement of gases in and out of the leaf
the leaf surfaces contain tiny holes called stomata	to absorb light
the leaf contains xylem and phloem tubes	to transport water and food

6 *Gunnera* is a plant with leaves that grow up to 130 cm in diameter.

Explain why it is an advantage for *Gunnera* to have such large leaves.   **[2 marks]**

_____

_____

7 Some students are carrying out an investigation to see how the amount of light a plant receives affects the rate of photosynthesis in pondweed.

They set up the apparatus shown in the diagram.

The pondweed produces bubbles of oxygen. The students count how many bubbles are produced in one minute at different distances from the lamp.

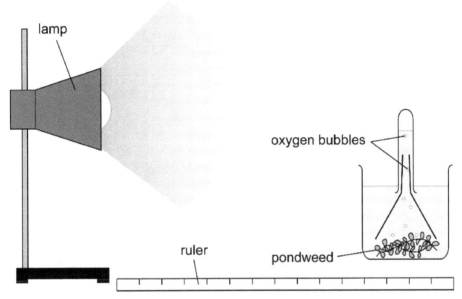

Apparatus used in an investigation to see the effect of light on photosynthesis.

a. Identify the variable that is being changed.   **[1 mark]**

_____

b. The students use the same piece of pondweed throughout the investigation. One student suggests that they should use a different piece of pondweed each time.

Select which method is best.

Tick one **box** and then explain your answer.   **[1 mark]**

use the same piece of pondweed each time   ☐

use a different piece of pondweed each time   ☐

Explanation _____

c. Explain why the students think that counting bubbles is a good way to measure photosynthesis.

[2 marks]

_____

_____

8 Every year huge areas of forest all around the world are being cut down.

Scientists are concerned that removing so many trees could change the balance of carbon dioxide and oxygen in the atmosphere.

Explain why scientists think removing forests is linked with changes in the levels of atmospheric carbon dioxide and oxygen.

[2 marks]

_____

_____

_____

Total marks _____ /16

Biology – Photosynthesis core

Biology – Photosynthesis

1 Why are plants called producers?

Tick **one** box. [1 mark]

Because they produce many leaves ☐

Because they reproduce quickly ☐

Because they can produce their own food using energy from light ☐

Because they take in nutrients from the soil to make wood ☐

2 Complete the word equation for photosynthesis. [2 marks]

_____ + water → glucose + _____

3 List **two** ways that plants use the glucose made in photosynthesis. [2 marks]

1 _____

2 _____

4 Draw **one** line from each adaptation of a leaf to the correct function. [2 marks]

Adaptation of leaf	Function
palisade cells are packed with chloroplasts filled with chlorophyll	to control the diffusion of gases in and out of the leaf
the upper and lower leaf surface contain stomata and guard cells	to absorb light
the leaf contains xylem and phloem tubes	to transport water and food

5 Giant aroid plants grow on the floor of tropical rainforests in Borneo. Their leaves can measure 3 m across.

Suggest why it is an advantage for the aroid plant to have such large leaves. [2 marks]

_____

_____

6 A student is carrying out an investigation to see how the amount of light a plant receives affects the rate of photosynthesis in pondweed.

He uses the apparatus shown in the diagram.

The student counts how many bubbles of oxygen are given off by the pondweed in one minute, at different distances from a lamp.

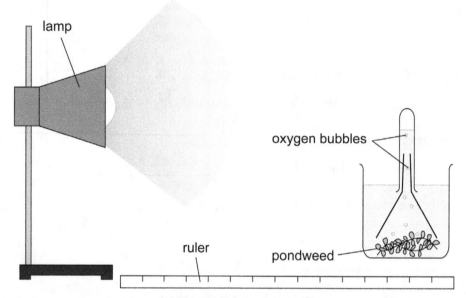

Apparatus used in an investigation to see the effect of light on photosynthesis.

a. Identify **two** variables the student should control to ensure his investigation is a fair test.

[2 marks]

1 _____

2 _____

b. Another student suggests that it would be better to measure the volume of oxygen produced rather than counting the bubbles.

Measuring the volume of oxygen given off is likely to produce more valid results than counting bubbles.

Give **one** reason why. [2 marks]

_____

_____

7 Every year huge areas of tropical rain forest are being deforested. Scientists are concerned that removing so many trees could affect the concentration of oxygen and carbon dioxide in the atmosphere.

a. Which statement predicts how the concentration of carbon dioxide and oxygen are most likely to change? Tick **one** box. [1 mark]

The concentration of carbon dioxide and oxygen will increase ☐

The concentration of carbon dioxide and oxygen will decrease ☐

The concentration of carbon dioxide will decrease and the level of oxygen will increase ☐

The concentration of carbon dioxide will increase and the level of oxygen will decrease ☐

b. Explain your answer to part **a**. [2 marks]

_____

_____

_____

_____

Total marks _____ /16

Biology – Evolution, extinction and biodiversity

1 Organisms that need similar resources may compete with each other if the resources are in short supply.

List **two** resources that animals may compete for. **[2 marks]**

1 _____

2 _____

2 Thousands of years ago, the ancestors of giraffes lived in Africa. Some had slightly longer necks than others.

They fed off leaves in the trees.

a. Describe the **variation** in the necks of the giraffes that existed long ago. **[1 mark]**

_____

b. The table contains statements about ancestors of the giraffe.

Complete the table to show whether the statements are true or false. **[3 marks]**

Statement	True	False
The length of a giraffe's neck was controlled by its genes.		
The offspring of giraffes with longer necks also had longer necks.		
The length of a giraffe's neck could change in its lifetime depending on the environment where it lived.		

c. Explain why it could be an advantage for a giraffe to have a longer neck. **[1 mark]**

_____

d. The diagram below shows how giraffes in Africa today have a longer neck than their ancestors.

modern giraffe

ancestor giraffe

Time

Complete the following sentences about how the giraffes changed over time.

Choose from these terms. [3 marks]

adapted   die   reproduce   natural selection   mutated   genetic screening

The giraffes that had genes for longer necks were better _____ to the environment and, therefore, were more likely to survive and _____. The genes that allowed these individuals to be successful were passed to their offspring. This process is called _____ and led to the evolution of the modern giraffe.

3   The golden toad was first discovered in the Monteverde cloud forest in Costa Rica. It hasn't been found anywhere else in the world.

Between 1987 and 1992, scientists recorded how many golden toads were observed.

The table shows the results.

Year	Number of golden toads observed by scientists
1987	1500
1988	1
1989	1
1990	0
1991	0
1992	0

a.   Based on the data collected, scientists claim the golden toad is extinct.

In what year does the data suggest the toads became extinct? [1 mark]

_____

b.   Identify the **evidence** supporting the claim that the toads are extinct. [1 mark]

_____

c. Which of the following is a possible reason that the golden toad became extinct?

Tick **one** box. [1 mark]

An increase in resources ☐

Change in habitat due to severe weather conditions ☐

Less competition for mates ☐

Less competition for habitats ☐

4 Scientists are now able to preserve the genetic material of a plant or animal that is endangered.

What name is given to a place where genetic material such as sperm, eggs or seeds can be stored for future use? [1 mark]

_____

5 Describe what is meant by the term *biodiversity*. [1 mark]

_____

6 Suggest one reason why it is important to maintain biodiversity on Earth. [1 mark]

_____

_____

Total marks _____ /16

Biology – Evolution, extinction and biodiversity

1 Which scientist is best known for his work on evolution?

   Tick **one** box.   [1 mark]

   James Watson ☐

   Robert Bakewell ☐

   Gregor Mendel ☐

   Charles Darwin ☐

2 Draw **one** line from each word to the correct definition.   [2 marks]

Word	Definition
adaptation	the differences that exist between individuals in a population
variation	change in structure or function of an organism to become more suited to an environment
competition	when organisms all need the same resources, which are in short supply

3 Theories of evolution have been based on studies of organisms' structure and genetic makeup, and through direct observation.

   Name **one** other important source of evidence that can tell us about organisms which lived in the past.

                                                                          [1 mark]

   _____

4 The golden toad was first discovered in the Monteverde cloud forest in Costa Rica. It hasn't been found anywhere else in the world.

Between 1987 and 1992, scientists recorded how many golden toads were observed.

The table shows their results.

Year	Number of golden toads observed by scientists
1987	1500
1988	1
1989	1
1990	0
1991	0
1992	0

a. In 1992, scientists concluded the golden toad was extinct.

What is meant by the term *extinct*? [1 mark]

_____

b. Identify the evidence that the golden toad is extinct. [1 mark]

_____

c. Suggest **one** reason that the golden toad became extinct. [1 mark]

_____

d. Describe **one** method that is used by scientists to preserve the genetic material of a plant or animal that is endangered. [1 mark]

_____

5 Variation within a species means that the species is less likely to become endangered or extinct if the climate changes.

Explain why. [1 mark]

_____

6 Describe what is meant by the term *biodiversity*. [1 mark]

_____

7 Suggest **one** reason why it is important to maintain biodiversity on Earth. [1 mark]

_____

_____

8 Lemmings are furry rodents that are found in the Arctic tundra.

In 1800 a population of lemmings was taken from the Arctic to an area with a warmer climate. The lemmings lived and reproduced in the new area.

The population of lemmings was revisited 200 years later.

Some information about the fur length of the lemmings is shown in the table.

Year	Average fur length (mm)
1800	12
2000	8

a. Describe what the data shows. [1 mark]

_____

b. Use the theory of natural selection to explain the data. [4 marks]

_____

_____

_____

_____

_____

_____

Total marks _____ /16

Biology – Genes and inheritance

1 Complete the following sentences. Choose from these words. **[2 marks]**

       DNA   **cytoplasm**   **offspring**   **grandparents**   **RNA**

Heredity is the passing on of genetic information from parents to _____ .
The genetic information is carried from one generation to the next by a molecule called

_____ .

2 The diagram shows the genetic material found inside the nucleus of a cell.

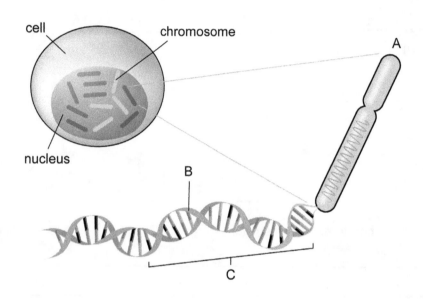

   a. Which letter shows a chromosome? **[1 mark]**

     _____

   b. Which letter shows DNA? **[1 mark]**

     _____

   c. **C** shows a section of genetic material that codes for a particular characteristic.

     What is the name of **C**? **[1 mark]**

     _____

3 Human body cells contain 46 chromosomes. Human sperm and egg cells only have 23 chromosomes.

Explain why. **[2 marks]**

_____

_____

4 A rat has 42 chromosomes in its body cells.

How many chromosomes does a rat have in its sex cells?

Tick **one** box. [1 mark]

21 ☐

42 ☐

84 ☐

5 The diagram shows two family trees.

Some people in the diagram carry the gene for being able to roll their tongue.

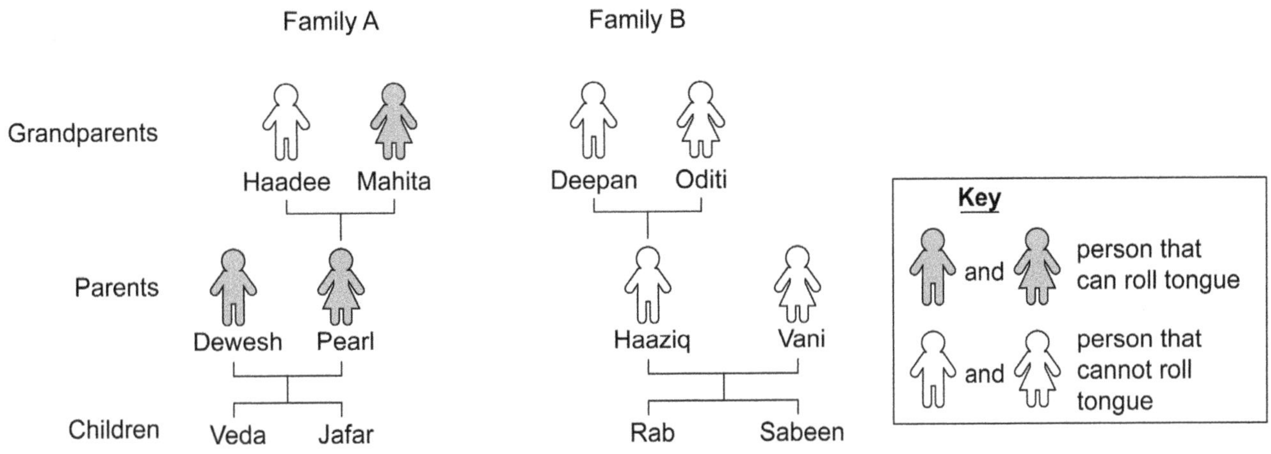

a. Identify **two children** who are most likely to be able to roll their tongues. [1 mark]

1 _____

2 _____

b. Explain why Haaziq cannot roll his tongue [2 marks]

_____

6 Polydactyly is a condition that results in humans having extra fingers or toes. It is caused by a gene mutation.

Explain why a parent with polydactyly might have a child with polydactyly. [2 marks]

_____

_____

7 In the 1940s scientists knew that DNA was an important molecule. However, they did not know about its structure.

In the 1950s, two scientists, Franklin and Wilkins, studied DNA using X-rays. Franklin and Wilkins were experts in a technique called X-ray diffraction.

Franklin produced an X-ray photograph that gave important clues about the structure of DNA. This allowed other scientists, Watson and Crick, to understand more about the physical structure of DNA

a. What question were all the scientists trying to answer?   **[1 mark]**

_____

b. Give **one** piece of evidence that Watson and Crick used to produce their DNA model.   **[1 mark]**

_____

c. Explain how the work of Watson and Crick was made possible by other scientists.   **[1 mark]**

_____

_____

Total marks _____ /16

Biology – Genes and inheritance

1   The diagram shows the genetic material found inside the nucleus of a cell.

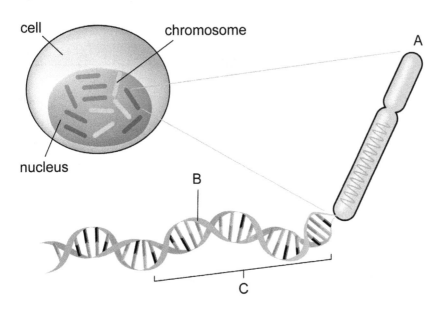

Name the parts labelled **A**, **B** and **C**. Choose from these words.   [3 marks]

base	chromosome	DNA	enzyme	gene	RNA

A _____

B _____

C _____

2   Complete the table to show if the following statements about DNA and genes are true or false.

Use a tick to show if a statement is true or false.   [3 marks]

Statement	True	False
DNA is only found in egg and sperm cells.		
DNA is made from two strands twisted together to make a double helix.		
A gene codes for a particular characteristic.		

3 The diagram show two families. Some people in the diagram have a gene that means they can role their tongue.

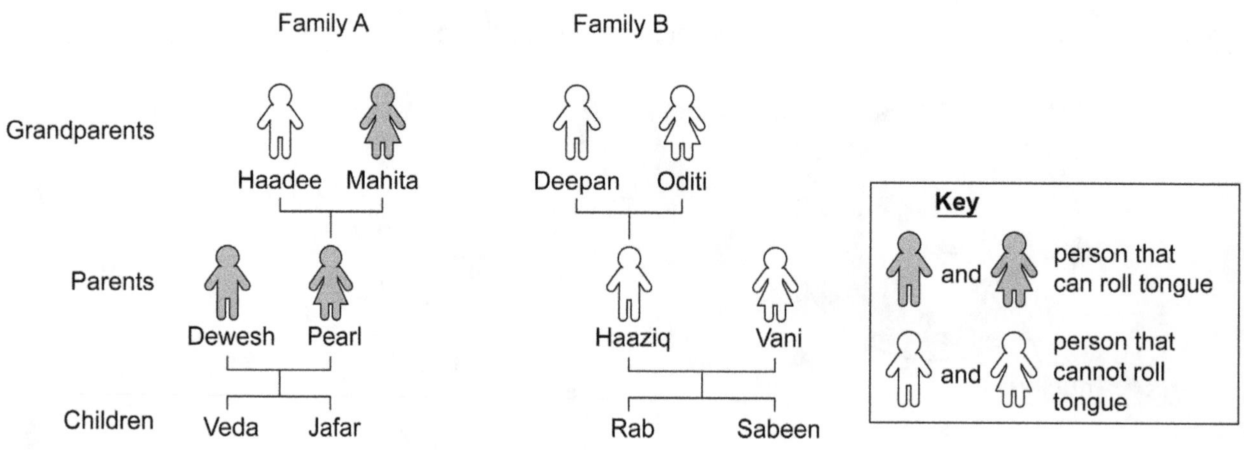

Family A

Family B

Grandparents   Haadee   Mahita   Deepan   Oditi

Key

person that can roll tongue

person that cannot roll tongue

Parents   Dewesh   Pearl   Haaziq   Vani

Children   Veda   Jafar   Rab   Sabeen

a. Identify **two** children who are most likely to be able to roll their tongues.   **[1 mark]**

1 _____

2 _____

b. Rab gets married to a woman who cannot roll her tongue. They have a child who also cannot roll their tongue.

Explain why.   **[2 marks]**

_____

_____

4 Complete the table to show the number of chromosomes in each type of cell from a rabbit.   **[2 marks]**

Type of cell in rabbit	Number of chromosomes found in nucleus of cell
skin cell	44
heart cell	
sex cell	

5 A man and a woman have two daughters. Although the daughters are sisters, they do not look identical.

Explain why.   **[2 marks]**

_____

_____

6 In the 1940s, scientists knew that DNA was a very important molecule. However, they did not know about its structure.

In the 1950s, two scientists, Franklin and Wilkins, studied DNA using X-rays. Franklin and Wilkins were experts in a technique called X-ray diffraction.

Franklin produced an X-ray diffraction photograph that gave important clues about the structure of DNA.

Meanwhile another scientist, Chargaff, discovered DNA contained the bases A, T, C and G.

This information allowed two other scientists, Watson and Crick, to produce a 3D model of the structure of DNA.

a. What question were all the scientists trying to answer? **[1 mark]**

_____

b. Give **two** pieces of evidence that Watson and Crick used to produce their model. **[2 marks]**

1 _____

2 _____

Total marks _____ /16

Chemistry – The Periodic Table

1 The diagram shows part of the Periodic Table of elements.

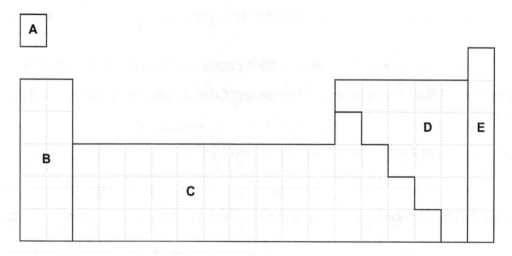

a. Which area contains a group of non-metals?

Write **one** letter.   [1 mark]

_____

b. Which areas contain only metals?

Write **two** letters.   [2 marks]

_____

c. Name the element found in box **A**.

_____   [1 mark]

d. The Periodic Table also contains several periods of elements.

Shade in a period of elements on the diagram.   [1 mark]

2 The table shows the melting points of some of the halogens.

Halogen	Melting point (°C)
fluorine	−219
chlorine	172
bromine	266
iodine	387

a. Which halogen has the highest melting point?

_____   [1 mark]

b. Bromine can be a **gas** or a **liquid** or a **solid**.

Complete the following sentence. [1 mark]

When bromine is heated from room temperature to 268°C, the bromine changes from a

_____ to a _____.

c. Predict how the boiling point of the halogens will change as you go down the group from fluorine to iodine.

Suggest a reason for your answer. [2 marks]

_____

_____

3 Look at Mendeleev's early version of the Periodic Table shown below.

Reihen	Gruppo I. — R'O	Gruppo II. — RO	Gruppo III. — R'O'	Gruppo IV. RH⁴ RO'	Gruppo V. RH³ R'O⁵	Gruppo VI. RH² RO'	Gruppo VII. RH R'O'	Gruppo VIII. — RO⁴
1	H=1							
2	Li=7	Be=9,4	B=11	C=12	N=14	O=16	F=19	
3	Na=23	Mg=24	Al=27,3	Si=28	P=31	S=32	Cl=35,5	
4	K=39	Ca=40	—=44	Ti=48	V=51	Cr=52	Mn=55	Fe=56, Co=59, Ni=59, Cu=63.
5	(Cu=63)	Zn=65	—=68	—=72	As=75	Se=78	Br=80	
6	Rb=85	Sr=87	?Yt=88	Zr=90	Nb=94	Mo=96	—=100	Ru=104, Rh=104, Pd=106, Ag=108.
7	(Ag=108)	Cd=112	In=113	Sn=118	Sb=122	Te=125	J=127	
8	Cs=133	Ba=137	?Di=138	?Ce=140	—	—	—	— — — —
9	(—)	—	—	—	—	—	—	
10	—	—	?Er=178	?La=180	Ta=182	W=184	—	Os=195, Ir=197, Pt=198, Au=199.
11	(Au=199)	Hg=200	Tl=204	Pb=207	Bi=208	—	—	
12	—	—	—	Th=231	—	U=240	—	— — — —

a. Compare this table with the modern Periodic Table. [2 marks]

_____

_____

b. Explain why Mendeleev left some gaps in the Periodic Table. [2 marks]

_____

_____

4 The graph shows the melting points and boiling points of some alkali metals.

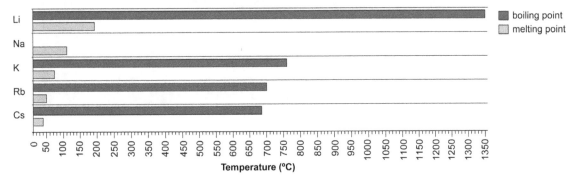

a. Describe the pattern in the melting points and the boiling points of the elements. [1 mark]

_____

b. Sketch a bar on the graph to show the approximate boiling point of sodium. [1 mark]

c. Fr is found in group 1 below Cs.

Fr is a solid at the standard temperature of 20°C.

Use the data on the graph to predict its melting point. [1 mark]

_____

Total marks _____ /16

Chemistry – The Periodic Table

1 The diagram shows an outline of the Periodic Table of elements.

   Five elements – **A**, **B**, **C**, **D** and **E** – are marked on the table.

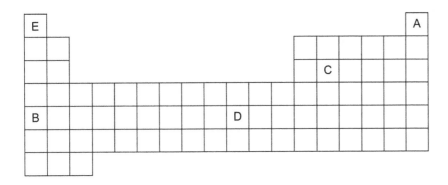

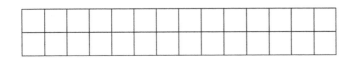

a. Identify an element you would use to fill a balloon.

   i. Write **one** letter. _____   [1 mark]

   ii. Give a reason for your answer.   [1 mark]

   _____

b. Identify an element you would use in a catalytic converter fitted to a car.

   i. Write **one** letter. _____   [1 mark]

   ii. Give a reason for your answer.   [1 mark]

   _____

c. The halogens are found in group 7 of the Periodic Table.

   Shade in group 7 in the table above.   [1 mark]

2 Some group 1 metals were dropped into a trough of water.

   The observations were recorded in a table.

Group 1 metal	Reaction with cold water
lithium	metal floated; it fizzed slowly until it disappeared
sodium	metal melted to form a ball; it fizzed rapidly until it disappeared
potassium	metal melted to form a ball; it fizzed violently, then set on fire and burned with a lilac flame and some sparks

a. Describe the trend in reactivity of the group 1 metals.

Use the observations recorded in the table to support your answer. **[2 marks]**

_____

_____

b. When a piece of freshly cut sodium metal is left in the air, the shiny surface goes dull.

Explain why. **[1 mark]**

_____

c. Complete the word equation for the chemical reaction taking place in part **b**. **[1 mark]**

sodium + oxygen → _____

d. Predict what you will see when a piece of freshly cut potassium is left in the air. **[1 mark]**

_____

_____

3 The graph shows the melting points and the boiling points of some halogens.

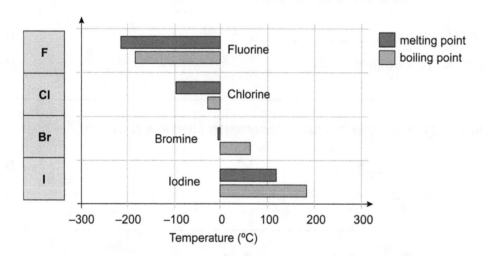

a. Describe the pattern in the melting points and boiling points of the elements. **[1 mark]**

_____

b. Use the data in the graph to explain why bromine is in the liquid state when stored in a sealed bottle at temperature at 20°C. **[2 marks]**

_____

_____

c. The element At is found below I in group 7 of the Periodic Table.

Predict **one physical** property of At. **[1 mark]**

_____

_____

d. A more reactive halogen will displace a less reactive halogen from a solution of its salt.

Identify the reaction that will take place.

Tick **one** box. [1 mark]

bromine + potassium fluoride ☐

fluorine + sodium iodide ☐

iodine + lithium bromide ☐

chlorine + sodium fluoride ☐

e. Write a word equation for the reaction taking place in part **d**. [1 mark]

_____

Total marks _____ /16

Chemistry – The Periodic Table extended

Chemistry – Materials

core

1 Complete the following sentences.

Choose from these terms.　**[3 marks]**

atom　　compound　　element　　mixture　　particle　　molecule　　solid

An _____ is a pure substance made up of only one type of atom.

A _____ is formed when two or more atoms join together.

If the atoms are different, then a _____ is formed.

2 A student put on her safety glasses. She then burned a piece of magnesium in a blue Bunsen burner flame.

She made the following observations:

- the magnesium burned with a bright white light

- at the end of the reaction there was a white powder.

a. Name the white powder.　**[1 mark]**

_____

The student put half of the white powder in a small beaker of water.

She added three drops of universal indicator.

b. Explain why the universal indicator went blue.　**[1 mark]**

_____

Finally, the student added some hydrochloric acid to the rest of the white powder.

When the reaction stopped she added three drops of universal indicator.

c. Explain why the universal indicator stayed green.　**[1 mark]**

_____

d. Complete the word equation.　**[1 mark]**

magnesium oxide + hydrochloric acid → _____ + _____

3 a. Name the acidic compound produced when carbon is burned in oxygen.　**[1 mark]**

_____

b. Complete the symbol equation.　**[1 mark]**

$C + O_2 \rightarrow$ _____

c. Complete the sentence.　**[1 mark]**

When universal indicator is added to nitrogen dioxide the colour changes from
_____ to _____.

4 Plastics are man-made polymers.

a. Define polymer. [1 mark]

_____

A student is investigating the strength of some plastic supermarket bags.

He gathers together the following equipment:

- clamp and stand
- weights
- ruler
- scissors
- plastic bags.

b. Design an experiment to investigate the strength of the plastic bags. [4 marks]

_____

_____

_____

_____

c. Identify the independent variable. [1 mark]

_____

Total marks _____ /16

Chemistry – Materials

1 The diagrams below show different combinations of atoms.

A
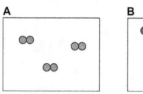

B
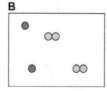

C
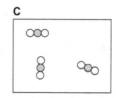

D
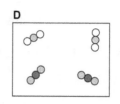

E
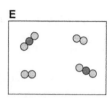

   a. Write down the letter of the diagram which shows a **pure** compound.   **[1 mark]**

   _____

   b. Write down the letter of the diagram which shows a mixture of **two** elements.   **[1 mark]**

   _____

   c. Write down the letter of the diagram which shows an element and a compound.   **[1 mark]**

   _____

   d. Write down the letter of the diagram which could represent carbon dioxide.   **[1 mark]**

   _____

   e. Suggest a name for the substance represented in diagram **A**.   **[1 mark]**

   _____

2 a. Complete the table.   **[4 marks]**

Name of oxide	Formula	When dissolved in water	
		Acidic	**Alkaline**
carbon dioxide	_____	yes	no
_____	MgO	_____	_____
calcium oxide	_____	no	yes
_____	SO_2	_____	_____

   b. When a metal oxide reacts with an acid, a salt and water are produced.

   Complete the symbol equation for the reaction of sulfuric acid and calcium oxide.   **[2 marks]**

   $H_2SO_4 + CaO \rightarrow$ _____ + _____

3 The table lists the properties of some materials.

Type of material	Material	Density (g/cm³)	Strength (MPa)*	Strength/weight ratio
composite	fibreglass	1.9	3400	1307
composite	carbon fibre	1.6	4300	2457
metal	aluminium	2.8	600	214
metal	stainless steel	7.86	2000	254
composite	concrete	2.3	12	4.35

* The pressure needed to squash the material until it breaks.

a. Badminton racquets used to be made from aluminium but now they are made from carbon fibre.

Use the data to suggest a reason why.   [1 mark]

_____

b. Choose a metal from the table that you would use to build the supports for a bridge.

Give a reason for your answer.   [2 marks]

_____

_____

Ceramics are used for many things including bricks, plates and floor tiles.

c. Explain why ceramics are used for plates.   [1 mark]

_____

d. Explain why ceramics are used for floor tiles.   [1 mark]

_____

Total marks _____ /16

Chemistry – Energetics

1   The diagram shows four pieces of equipment used to make measurements.

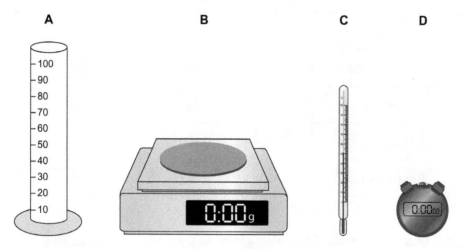

    A   B   C   D

a.   Identify the piece of equipment used to measure energy changes.

Write **one** letter.

_____   **[1 mark]**

b.   Complete the sentences.   **[2 marks]**

Choose from these terms.

lower   higher   exothermic   endothermic   temperature

In an _____ reaction energy is given out usually as heat or light.
The temperature at the end of the reaction is _____ than at the start.

2   When a substance changes state, there is also a change in internal energy.

Draw **one** line from each change of state to its energy change.   **[4 marks]**

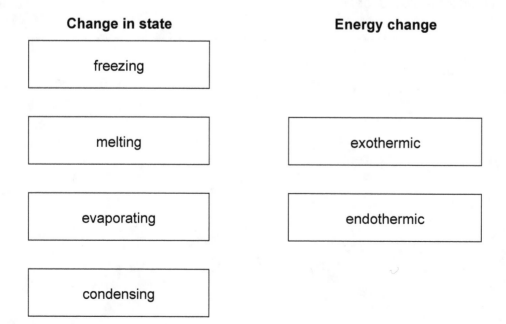

3 Two students were investigating the energy changes in different chemical reactions.

Their results are recorded in the table.

Reaction	Temperature at start (°C)	Temperature at end (°C)	Change in temperature (°C)
sodium ethanoate and water	20.0	48.2	_____
citric acid and hydrogen sodium carbonate	20.0	17.8	_____

a. Calculate the change in temperature and complete the table. [2 marks]

b. Use the data in the table to choose which reaction would be better for hand warmers.

Give a reason for your answer. [2 marks]

_____

_____

c. Identify the endothermic reaction.

Give a reason for your answer. [2 marks]

_____

_____

4 a. A catalyst is a substance that is added to a chemical reaction ...

Complete the sentence above.

Tick **one** box. [1 mark]

... to make it smell nice. ☐

... to speed up the reaction without changing the reactants. ☐

... to give it more energy. ☐

... to lower the temperature. ☐

Chemistry – Energetics core

Hydrogen peroxide decomposes to produce oxygen gas and water.

The graph shows the reaction with and without a catalyst.

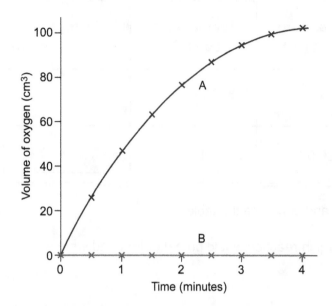

b. Determine which reaction had a catalyst.

Tick **one** box. [1 mark]

A ☐

B ☐

c. Give a reason for your answer to part **b**. [1 mark]

_____

Total marks _____ /16

Chemistry – Energetics

1   Complete the sentences below.

Choose from these terms.   [3 marks]

exothermic   made   endothermic   broken   released   formed

During a chemical reaction bonds are _____ and new bonds are formed.

Energy is needed to break bonds, but it is _____ when the new bonds are formed.
If the energy released is less than the energy required, the reaction is _____.

2   When magnesium metal is heated in a Bunsen flame, light energy is given out.

   a.   Complete the symbol equation for the reaction.   [2 marks]

        $2Mg + O_2 \rightarrow$ _____

The graph shows how the energy levels of the reactants and products change during the reaction.

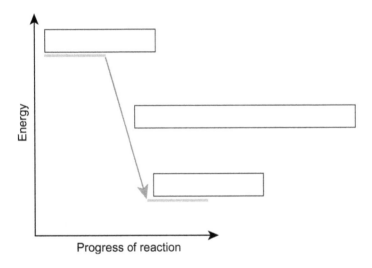

   b.   Label the graph.

        Choose from these terms.   [3 marks]

        2MgO   heat is released   heat is taken in $2Mg + O_2$

   c.   Describe what happens to the chemical bonds during the reaction.   [2 marks]

        _____

        _____

   d.   Describe how the graph would change if the reaction were endothermic.   [2 marks]

        _____

        _____

3 Two students put some ice in a beaker and then heated it.

They recorded the temperature every minute for 15 minutes.

The graph shows their results.

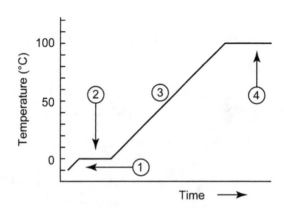

Use the graph to answer the questions.

a. Name the type of energy change taking place at step 2.

Give a reason for your answer.   **[2 marks]**

_____

_____

b. Explain what is happening to the particles at step 4.   **[2 marks]**

_____

_____

Total marks _____ **/16**

Chemistry – Chemical reactions

1 When a fuel burns a chemical reaction takes place.

   a. Name the reaction type.

      Tick **two** boxes.   **[2 marks]**

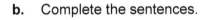

         Displacement ☐

         Combustion ☐

         Oxidation ☐

         Thermal decomposition ☐

   b. Complete the sentences.   **[3 marks]**

      Choose from these terms.

           oxygen   **carbon**   **nitrogen**   **hydrogen**   **water**

      Fuels such as oil and gas contain the elements _____ and _____.
      They are called hydrocarbons. When they burn in oxygen, carbon dioxide and
      _____ are formed.

Look at the equations for the reaction of carbon and oxygen.

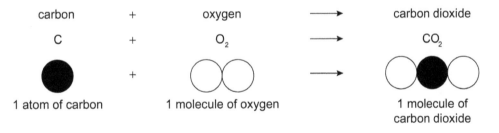

carbon	+	oxygen	⟶	carbon dioxide
C	+	O_2	⟶	CO_2
1 atom of carbon	+	1 molecule of oxygen	⟶	1 molecule of carbon dioxide

   c. Describe what happens to the atoms during the reaction.   **[1 mark]**

      _____

   d. Explain what is meant by the law of conservation of mass.   **[2 marks]**

      _____

      _____

2 Look at the diagram.

Before the reaction   After the reaction

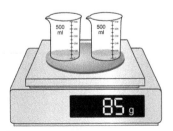 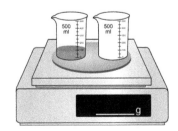

a. Write down the mass after the reaction. [1 mark]

_____ g

b. Explain your answer to part **a**. [2 marks]

_____

_____

3 When magnesium burns in air the mass of the solid increases.

The equation for the reaction is:

magnesium + oxygen → magnesium oxide

$\quad$ 2Mg $\quad$ + $\quad$ O_2 $\quad$ → $\quad$ 2MgO

a. Suggest a reason why there is an 'increase in mass' during the reaction. [2 marks]

_____

_____

b. 12 g of magnesium reacts with 8 g of oxygen.

Calculate the mass of magnesium oxide produced. [1 mark]

_____

4 An iodine crystal was placed in a sealed flask.

The flask was weighed and the mass was recorded.

After 10 minutes the flask was filled with a purple gas. The flask was weighed again.

a. Predict whether the new mass increased, stayed the same or decreased. [1 mark]

Tick **one** box.

It increased. ☐

It stayed the same. ☐

It decreased. ☐

b. Suggest a reason for your answer to part **a**. [1 mark]

_____

_____

Total marks _____ /16

Chemistry – Chemical reactions core

Chemistry – Chemical reactions

1 When a metal carbonate is heated to a high temperature a chemical change takes place.

    a. Name the reaction type.

        Tick **one** box.   **[1 mark]**

            Displacement   ☐

            Combustion   ☐

            Oxidation   ☐

            Thermal decomposition ☐

    The diagram shows the apparatus used to heat some copper carbonate.

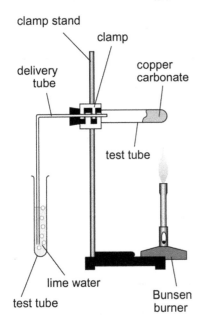

    b. Write down **one** safety precaution that should be taken.   **[1 mark]**

    _____

    c. Describe **one** change you would expect to see during the experiment.   **[1 mark]**

    _____

    _____

    d. Complete the equation for the reaction.   **[1 mark]**

        $CuCO_3$ (s) $\rightarrow$ CuO (s) + _____ (g)

The test tube and its contents were weighed at the start and at the end of the experiment.

The results are recorded in the table.

Mass of test tube and contents at the start (g)	32.5
Mass of test tube and contents at the end (g)	28.1
Change in mass of test tube and contents during the reaction (g)	_____

e. Calculate the change in mass the occurring during the reaction and complete the table. **[1 mark]**

f. Use the law of conservation of mass to explain your answer to part **e**. **[3 marks]**

_____

_____

_____

_____

2 Ethanol is a fuel.

The chemical formula for ethanol is C_2H_5OH.

When ethanol burns in oxygen, heat is released to the surroundings.

a. Name the elements present in ethanol. **[1 mark]**

_____

b. Predict the products of the combustion reaction of ethanol. **[2 marks]**

_____

_____

c. Explain why this reaction is also an oxidation reaction. **[1 mark]**

_____

_____

3 A class investigated the reaction between metals and salt solutions.

They put a drop of salt solution in a dimple tray and then added a piece of metal.

The results are recorded in the table.

	Salt solution		
	$MgCl_2$	$CuCl_2$	$ZnCl_2$
Mg	✗	✓	✓
Cu	✗	✗	✗
Zn	✗	✓	✗

a. Compare the reactivity of the metals.

Use the information in the table. [2 marks]

_____

_____

b. Write a symbol equation for the reaction between magnesium and copper chloride. [2 marks]

_____

Total marks _____ /16

Chemistry – Chemical reactions extended

Chemistry – The atmosphere

1 The Earth's atmosphere consists of gases.

The table lists the percentages of the main gases in the Earth's atmosphere.

Gas	Percentage
nitrogen	78
oxygen	21
other (including argon, carbon dioxide and water)	1

a. Draw a bar chart to show the composition of the Earth's atmosphere.

Label the axes.   **[3 marks]**

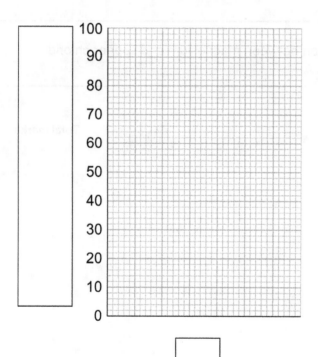

b. Identify the gas that makes up the largest percentage of the atmosphere.   **[1 mark]**

_____

c. Write down the formula for nitrogen gas.   **[1 mark]**

_____

d. Suggest a reason why the amount of water vapour in the air varies.   **[1 mark]**

_____

2 Carbon is found in all living organisms. It is recycled through the carbon cycle.

The diagram shows the carbon cycle.

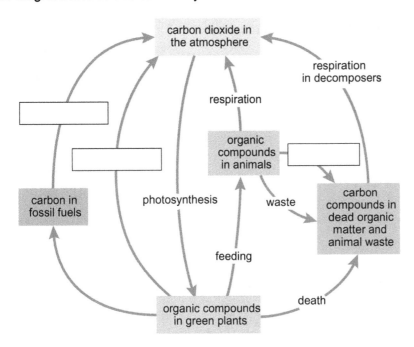

a. Complete the diagram of the carbon cycle.

Choose from these terms. **[3 marks]**

combustion   respiration   feeding   photosynthesis   death

b. Name the process that removes carbon from the air. **[1 mark]**

_____

c. Describe how a carbon atom from a dog could be found in a tree. **[3 marks]**

_____

_____

_____

_____

d. Describe **one** human activity that could disrupt the carbon cycle. **[1 mark]**

_____

_____

e. The greenhouse effect is a natural phenomenon that allows the Earth to be kept warm enough to support life.

Explain why scientists are concerned about the increasing amount of carbon dioxide in the atmosphere. **[2 marks]**

_____

_____

_____

Total marks _____ /16

Chemistry – The atmosphere core

Chemistry – The atmosphere

1 The pie chart shows the composition of the Earth's atmosphere.

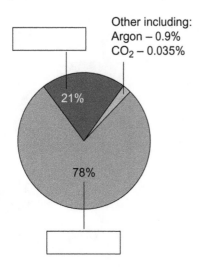

Other including:
Argon – 0.9%
CO_2 – 0.035%

21%

78%

   a. Label the pie chart.   **[2 marks]**

   b. The Earth's population is growing fast.

        Suggest **one** way this could impact on the composition of the atmosphere.   **[2 marks]**

        _____

        _____

        _____

2 Carbon is found in all living organisms. It is recycled through the carbon cycle.

    The diagram shows the carbon cycle.

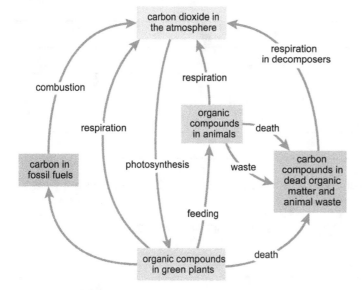

   a. Identify **two** processes that put carbon into the atmosphere.   **[1 mark]**

        _____

        _____

b. Describe how carbon is recycled around the environment through living things. **[3 marks]**

_____

_____

_____

_____

3 The graph shows how the Earth's climate has changed over the last 1000 years.

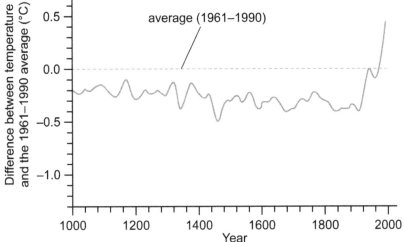

a. Describe what the graph shows. **[2 marks]**

_____

_____

b. Scientific research shows that human activities could be responsible for the changes that have occurred in the last 200 years.

Explain how human activities could be responsible for these changes. **[4 marks]**

_____

_____

_____

_____

c. Suggest **two** ways to minimise or reverse the trend in climate change. **[2 marks]**

_____

_____

_____

_____

Total marks _____ /16

Chemistry – The Earth's resources

1 a. Draw **one** line from each term to the correct definition. [2 marks]

Term	Definition
recycle	use less to avoid waste
reduce	use the object again
reuse	make new materials from old ones

b. Describe **two** ways in which councils help people to recycle more. [2 marks]

_____

_____

c. Suggest a reason why people need to recycle more. [1 mark]

_____

2 a. Complete the sentences.

Choose from these terms. [4 marks]

        mined   easier   harder   extracted

        electrolysis   oxidise   displace

Most metals exist in nature as compounds. To obtain a pure metal it must be
_____ from the metal compound. The more reactive the metal, the
_____ it is to separate.

Carbon is used to _____ less reactive metals but _____
is used to separate more reactive metals from their compounds.

b. Lead oxide is mixed with carbon and heated.

At the end of the reaction a silvery metal is observed.

Complete the word equation for the reaction. [2 marks]

lead oxide + carbon → _____ + _____

c. Which is the more reactive element in the reaction in part **b**?

Tick **one** box. [1 mark]

lead ☐   carbon ☐

d. Give a reason for your answer to part **c**. [1 mark]

_____

_____

3 The table gives data about the energy needed to recycle some materials.

Material	Reduction in energy needed to recycle rather than use raw material (%)
aluminium	96
glass	21
plastic	76
newsprint	45

a. Aluminium is a reactive metal.

Explain why it is efficient to recycle aluminium metal. [2 marks]

_____

_____

_____

b. Glass bottles are often reused rather than recycled.

Suggest a reason why. [1 mark]

_____

_____

Total marks _____ /16

Chemistry – The Earth's resources

1   Some metals are listed in order of decreasing reactivity.

    Potassium
    Magnesium
    Aluminium
    (Carbon)
    Zinc
    Nickel
    Tin
    Lead
    Copper
    Gold

a.   Name a metal that exists in nature as a pure metal.   [1 mark]

_____

b.   Carbon is a non-metal.

     Explain why it is included in the list.   [1 mark]

_____

c.   Draw **one** line from each metal to the most appropriate method of extracting it
     from its ore.   [2 marks]

Metal	Extraction method
copper	blast furnace
iron	electrolysis
potassium	roasting in air

d.   Describe how you might extract a sample of nickel from its ore.   [3 marks]

_____

_____

_____

_____

e. Aluminium is a very useful metal but it is very expensive to extract aluminium from its ore.

Explain why. **[4 marks]**

_____

_____

_____

_____

_____

f. Suggest a reason why the recycling of aluminium is an important industry. **[1 mark]**

_____

_____

2 The Earth supplies all our raw materials but these resources are limited.

Many of the products we use every day are made from plastics.

The table shows the energy required to produce some plastics.

Plastic	Energy required to produce plastic from raw materials (MJ/kg)	Energy required to recycle plastic (MJ/kg)
high density poly(ethene) (HDPE)	77–85	35–45
poly(propene) (PP)	77–83	35–45
polystyrene (PS)	96–105	40–50

a. Compare the energy efficiency of making the plastics from raw materials with the energy efficiency of recycling the plastics. **[2 marks]**

_____

_____

_____

b. Approximately 90% of the plastic used each year is made from raw materials. The remaining 10% is made from recycled plastics.

Suggest **two** reasons why recycled plastics are not used more widely. **[2 marks]**

_____

_____

_____

Total marks _____ /16

Chemistry – The Earth's resources extended

Physics – Sound

1 Complete the following sentences. Use words from the list.   **[3 marks]**

   vacuum   medium   vibration   transverse   longitudinal

   A sound is produced by a _____.

   A sound wave travels in the same line as the vibrations of the source. We say it is a
   _____ wave.

   Sound requires a _____ to travel through.

2 The diagrams below show the oscilloscope output for four sound waves.

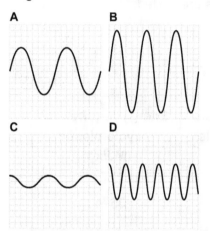

   Write **one** letter in each box.   **[3 marks]**

   State which graph shows:

   the largest amplitude   ☐

   the longest wavelength   ☐

   the highest frequency   ☐

3 A 14-year-old student and has good hearing.

   Identify the sounds that the student should be able to hear.

   Tick as many boxes as you need.   **[2 marks]**

   The note middle C on a piano (frequency = 260 Hz)   ☐

   The lowest note on a church organ (frequency = 8 Hz)   ☐

   The call of a bat (frequency = 45 kHz)   ☐

   The siren on a police car (frequency = 600 to 900 Hz)   ☐

   A dog whistle (frequency = 26 kHz)   ☐

   The highest note on a cymbal (frequency = 5 kHz)   ☐

4 Construction workers use pile drivers to build the foundations for large buildings. Pile drivers are very loud and a worker can spend most of the day using them.

    a. Explain why their work might damage their hearing.   **[2 marks]**

_____

_____

    b. Suggest **one** way they can protect their hearing.   **[1 mark]**

_____

5 The table shows the speed of sound waves in different materials.

Material	vacuum	air	water	steel
Speed of sound (m/s)	cannot be measured	343	1482	5960

    a. Explain why the speed of sound is higher in steel than in air.   **[2 marks]**

_____

_____

_____

_____

    b. An engineer is designing a system to warn people that a train is approaching. She uses a microphone to detect the sound of the train.

    Suggest the best place to put the microphone. Tick **one** box.   **[1 mark]**

        In the air, close to one side of the metal rails   ☐

        In the air, far away from the metal rails   ☐

        In contact with the metal rails   ☐

        In the ground, buried underneath the metal rails   ☐

6 Sound waves can be used to clean a small object.

The object is placed in a liquid. The liquid is then vibrated using ultrasonic waves.

The vibrations cause dirt to shake loose from the surface of the object.

    a. Explain what 'ultrasonic' means.   **[1 mark]**

_____

    b. Describe **one** other use of ultrasonic waves.   **[1 mark]**

_____

Total marks _____ /16

Physics – Sound

1 The diagram shows the oscilloscope trace of a sound wave.

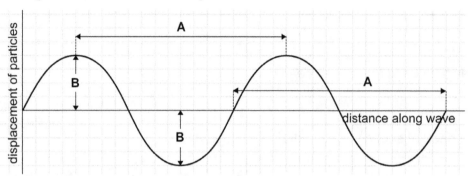

a. Write the correct labels for the quantities **A** and **B**. [2 marks]

A _____

B _____

b. Sound is a **longitudinal** wave that moves through a **medium**.

Define the words in **bold** text. [2 marks]

_____

_____

2 The diagrams below show the oscilloscope output for four sound waves.

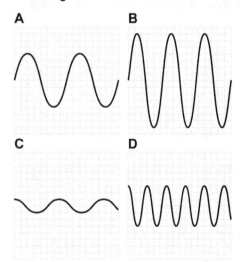

a. Write **one** letter in each box.

State which graph shows: [2 marks]

The longest wavelength ☐

The highest frequency ☐

b. Estimate the ratio of amplitudes **C** : **D**. [1 mark]

_____

Physics – Sound extended

3 A man is 70 years old and retired. He used to work as a 'roadie' (someone who sets up and takes apart the musical instruments and equipment at rock concerts).

He has his hearing tested and finds he cannot hear sounds above 1 kHz.

a. Write the name of the quantity that is measured using kHz. [1 mark]

_____

b. Give the range of hearing that an average person with healthy hearing should be able to hear. [1 mark]

_____

c. Suggest **one** reason why the 70-year-old man cannot hear the full, normal range of hearing. [1 mark]

_____

4 The table shows the speed of sound waves in different materials.

Material	vacuum	air	water	steel
Speed of sound (m/s)	cannot be measured	343	1482	5960

a. Explain why the speed of sound is higher in steel than in air. [2 marks]

_____

_____

b. Explain why the speed of sound cannot be measured in a vacuum. [1 mark]

_____

c. At room temperature, mercury is a liquid metal. Predict the speed of sound in mercury. [1 mark]

_____

5 A student sets up an experiment in a classroom to estimate the speed of sound using two microphones and an oscilloscope.

The diagram shows the apparatus he uses.

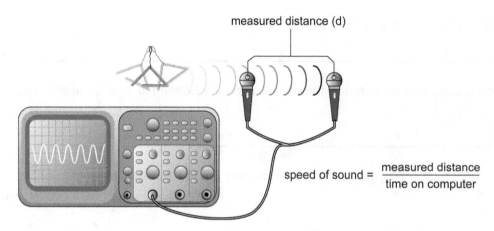

measured distance (d)

$$\text{speed of sound} = \frac{\text{measured distance}}{\text{time on computer}}$$

a. Explain why it is important to set up this experiment in a quiet room. **[1 mark]**

_____

_____

The student makes a loud sound. The diagram below shows the trace on the oscilloscope from **one** of the microphones.

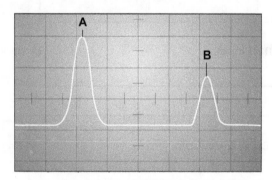

Peak **A** shows the sound the student made.

b. Identify what causes peak **B**. **[1 mark]**

_____

_____

Total marks _____ /16

Physics – Contact forces, moments and pressure

1 Complete the fraction in the equation for pressure.   **[1 mark]**

pressure = $\dfrac{\text{...}}{\text{...}}$

2 The diagram shows a book resting on a table. The arrow shows the force of the book's weight.

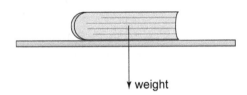

weight

a. Draw an arrow to show the reaction force of the table and where it acts.   **[1 mark]**

b. The book and the table are in equilibrium. Explain what this means.   **[1 mark]**

_____

_____

3 The diagram shows two force diagrams.

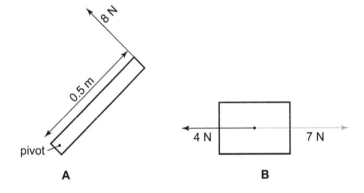

A   B

a. Object **A** is fixed at one end to a pivot. Describe what will happen to object **A**.   **[1 mark]**

_____

_____

b. Calculate the size and direction of the resultant force in **B**.   **[2 marks]**

_____

_____

4   A student carries out an experiment to measure the extension of a spring as it is loaded with different masses.

The results are shown in the table.

Mass m added (g)	L = Total length of spring (cm)	C = Original (unloaded) length of spring (cm)	Extension $y = L - C$ (cm)
0	20.0	20.0	0.0
100	21.5	20.0	1.5
200	23.0	20.0	3.0
300	24.6	20.0	3.6
400	26.1	20.0	6.1

a.   There is an error in the results table. Identify the error.   [1 mark]

_____

b.   Calculate the correct value.   [1 mark]

_____

The diagram shows an incomplete graph of the results of the extension y plotted against the mass m.

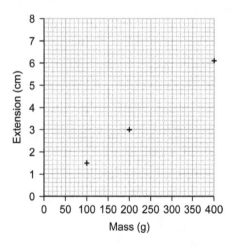

c.   Using your corrected value from part **b**, complete the graph.

Draw a line of best fit.   [2 marks]

d.   Does the spring obey Hooke's law?

Tick **one** box.   [1 mark]

Yes ☐

No ☐

5 Two skydivers jump out of a plane.

a. Explain what causes the skydivers to accelerate towards the ground. **[1 mark]**

_____

_____

b. One of them opens their parachute first. Explain why they start to travel more slowly than the other skydiver. **[2 marks]**

_____

_____

_____

_____

c. Our ears are very sensitive to the pressure of the air. As the skydivers fall, they can feel the pressure inside their ears increasing.

Explain their observation. **[2 marks]**

_____

_____

_____

_____

Total marks _____ /16

Physics – Contact forces, moments and pressure

1   The diagram below shows a book resting on a table in equilibrium.

    Draw arrows to show the forces acting on the book.   **[2 marks]**

2   The diagram below shows two force diagrams for objects **A** and **B**.

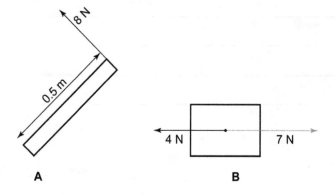

A   **B**

a.   Object **A** is fixed at one end to a pivot. Calculate the moment acting on **A**.   **[2 marks]**

_____

_____

b.   Determine the size and direction of the force needed to bring **B** into equilibrium.   **[2 marks]**

_____

_____

3 A student carries out an experiment to measure the extension of a spring as it is loaded with different masses.

The results are shown in the table.

Mass m added (g)	Total length of spring, L (cm)	Original (unloaded) length of spring, C (cm)	Extension $y = L - C$ (cm)
0	20.0	20.0	0.0
100	21.5	20.0	1.5
200	23.0	20.0	3.0
300	24.6	20.0	3.6
400	26.1	20.0	6.1

a. There is an error in the results table. Identify the error. **[1 mark]**

_____

b. Calculate the correct value. **[1 mark]**

_____

c. Using suitable axes and your corrected value from part **b**, plot the data from the table. **[3 marks]**

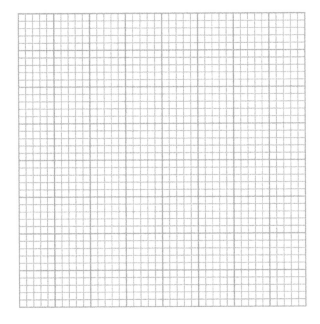

d. Draw a line of best fit. **[1 mark]**

e. Use your graph to determine whether or not the spring obeys Hooke's law. Justify your answer. **[2 marks]**

_____

_____

4   Most people can dive to depths of a few metres wearing just swimming costumes. Some underwater divers use breathing apparatus and protective suits to dive to much greater depths.

Using your knowledge of pressure, explain why divers need protective suits.   **[2 marks]**

_____

_____

_____

_____

Total marks _____ /16

Physics – Light

1 Choose whether each of these statements about the properties of light is true or false.

Tick **one** box for **each** statement. [4 marks]

Statement	True	False
Light only travels in straight lines.	☐	☐
An opaque object lets most of the light through.	☐	☐
A translucent object lets some of the light through.	☐	☐
A transparent object lets no light through.	☐	☐

2 The diagram shows an object placed in front of a mirror, with two rays of light from the object as they travel towards the mirror.

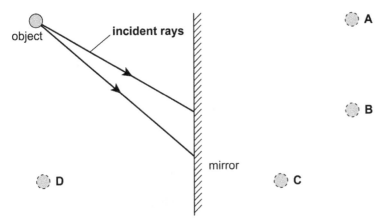

a. Draw the two rays of light after they have reflected from the mirror. [2 marks]

b. Determine where the image of the object will form.

Tick **one** box only. [1 mark]

At point **A** ☐

At point **B** ☐

At point **C** ☐

At point **D** ☐

3 Describe how the human eye works. You should include all the words in the list in your description.

The first sentence is written for you. **[2 marks]**

image   retina   lens   focuses

Light rays travel from a distant object to the eye.

_____

_____

4 The diagram shows light shining at an angle onto a transparent glass block.

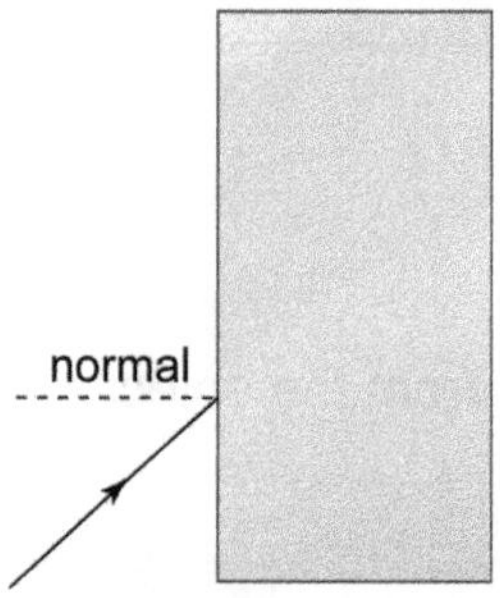

Complete the following sentences. Use words from the list. **[4 marks]**

slower   faster   reflection   refraction

normal   parallel   towards   away from

As the light enters the block, light rays bend _____ the normal.

Compared to the speed through air, light travels _____ through the block.

When the light ray leaves the block and enters the air again, it bends _____ the normal.

This bending of light is called _____ .

5   A student investigated how colour filters affected what she could see.

She placed different coloured objects on a table.

She looked at each object through different coloured filters.

The table shows her results.

Object colour	Filter colour	Colour seen
white	red	red
white	green	green
red	red	red
red	green	black
green	red	black
green	green	green

The student wrote some explanations for her investigation.

Use **only** the student's evidence to decide whether each explanation is correct, incorrect, or you cannot tell.

Tick the correct box for each conclusion.   **[3 marks]**

Conclusion	Correct	Incorrect	Cannot tell
White light passes through colour filters unaffected	☐	☐	☐
Red light passes through red filters but not through green filters	☐	☐	☐
A blue filter is needed to block both red and green light.	☐	☐	☐

Total marks _____ /16

Physics – Light

1 The diagrams shows light rays interacting with different materials.

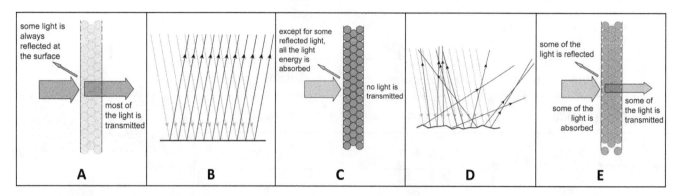

Match each image to the description of the process it shows.

Write **one** letter in each box.   **[5 marks]**

Description	Image
Scattering	☐
Specular reflection	☐
Opaque	☐
Translucent	☐
Transparent	☐

2 The diagram shows an object placed in front of a mirror with two rays of light from the object as they travel towards the mirror.

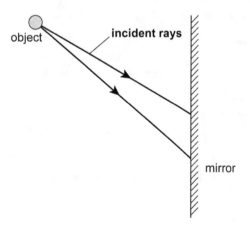

a. Draw the two rays of light after they have reflected from the mirror.   **[2 marks]**

b. Use dotted lines to determine where the image of the object will form.

Mark the location of the image clearly.   **[3 marks]**

3 The diagram shows light shining at an angle onto a transparent glass block.

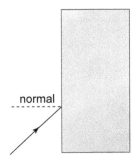

a. The light is refracted where it meets the glass. Draw the refracted ray. [1 mark]

b. Add a dashed line to show the normal where the refracted ray leaves the glass block. [1 mark]

c. The light is refracted again where it leaves the glass. Draw this second refracted ray. [1 mark]

4 A student investigated how colour filters affected what she could see.

She placed different coloured objects on a table.

She looked at each object through different coloured filters.

The table shows her results.

Object colour	Filter colour	Colour seen
white	red	red
white	green	green
red	red	red
red	green	Black
green	red	Black
green	green	green

a. Explain why the red object looks black when viewed through a green filter. [1 mark]

_____

_____

b. Predict what colour the student would see if she viewed a green object through a green filter.

Justify your answer. [2 marks]

_____

_____

Total marks _____ /16

Physics – Light extended

Physics – Magnetism and electromagnetism

1 Complete the sentences about magnetism.

Use terms from the list. **[4 marks]**

> **contact**   **non-contact**   **one pole**   **two poles**   **attract**   **repel**

Magnetic forces are _____ forces.

All magnets have _____ .

A north pole of one magnet will _____ the north pole of another magnet.

A north pole of one magnet will _____ the south pole of another magnet.

2 A student brings one pole of one magnet close to one pole of another magnet.

The magnets push away from each other.

Choose which of these statements could explain this observation.

Tick **all** the statements that could be correct. **[1 mark]**

Both poles are south poles, so they repel. ☐

One is a north pole, the other is a south pole, so they repel. ☐

All magnetic poles repel. ☐

Both poles are north poles, so they repel. ☐

3 The diagram shows two bar magnets and the magnetic field lines between them.

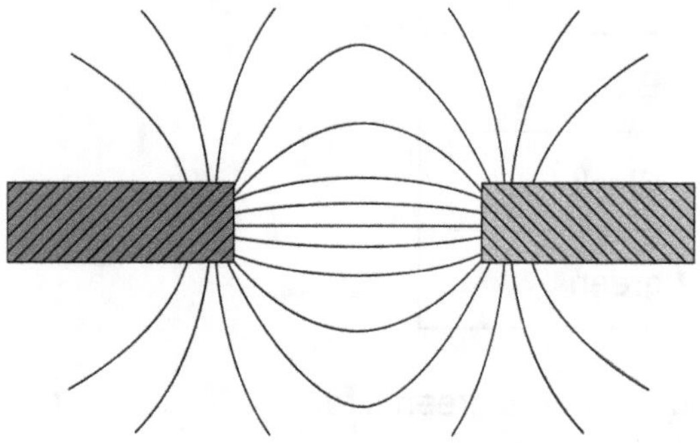

  a. The magnets attract each other. Label the north and south poles of both magnets. **[1 mark]**

  b. The magnetic field is shown but the direction is not labelled. Complete the diagram by adding arrowheads to all the field lines to show the direction of the field. **[1 mark]**

4 Describe **two** items of evidence that show the Earth behaves like a giant magnet. **[2 marks]**

  1 _____

  2 _____

5 The diagram shows the important working parts of a circuit breaker.

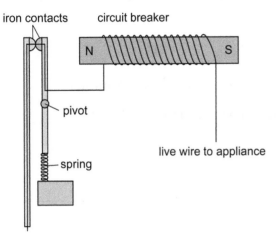

iron contacts   circuit breaker

N   S

pivot

live wire to appliance

spring

Complete the sentences that describe how this circuit breaker works.

Use words from the list. You may have to use some words more than once.   **[3 marks]**

breaks   low   weak   strong   high   completes

In normal operation, a _____ current passes through the electromagnet.

The magnetic field is _____ and the iron contacts stay touching.

If the current gets too _____, the magnetic field becomes _____ and the contacts separate.

This _____ the circuit.

6 In a science lesson, you are given the following apparatus:

   battery

   crocodile clips

   length of wire

   magnetic compass.

a. Explain how you could use this apparatus to show that an electrical current produces a magnetic field.   **[2 marks]**

_____

_____

b. You are given a sheet of paper and a pencil. Explain how you could use them with the compass to draw the shape and direction of the magnetic field around the wire.   **[2 marks]**

_____

_____

Total marks _____ /16

Physics – Magnetism and electromagnetism core

Physics – Magnetism and electromagnetism

1 Complete the following sentences. Use words from the list. **[4 marks]**

> **contact**   **non-contact**   **magnetic**   **electric**   **gravitational**

Static electricity, magnetism and gravity all create forces that are examples of _____ forces.

The charges on particles create the _____ force.

The attraction between an object and the Earth due to mass is the _____ force.

Another force involves north and south poles. This is called the _____ force.

2 The diagram shows two bar magnets.

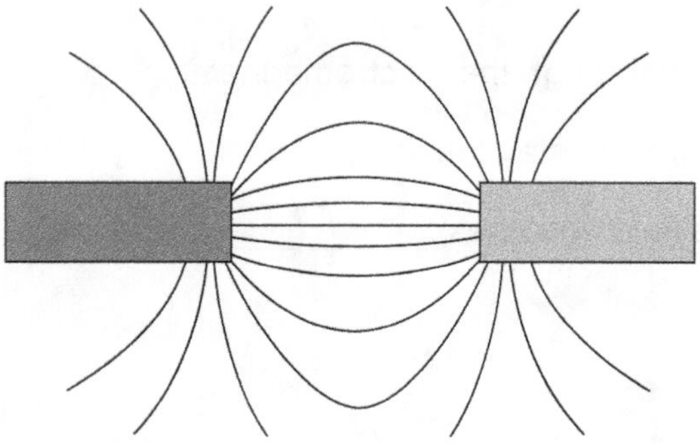

    a. The magnets attract each other. Label the north and south poles of both magnets. **[1 mark]**

    b. The magnetic field is shown but the direction is not labelled.

        Complete the diagram by adding arrowheads to all the field lines to show the direction of the field. **[1 mark]**

3 The Earth behaves like a giant magnet.

    a. Describe how you can show that the Earth has a magnetic field. **[1 mark]**

        _____

        _____

    b. State whether the magnetic pole at the geographical north of Earth is a magnetic north or south pole. **[1 mark]**

        _____

4   The diagram shows a length of straight wire at right-angles to a flat sheet of white paper.

The wire is connected to a power supply, which is then turned on.

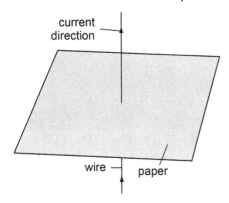

a.   Describe how you could use iron filings to show the magnetic field lines.   **[1 mark]**

_____

_____

The diagram shows a solenoid (a tightly-wound coil of wire). This acts like a bar magnet.

b.   Sketch the magnetic field lines on the diagram. Make sure you include the direction of the field using arrows.   **[3 marks]**

5   The diagram shows a simple electromagnet.

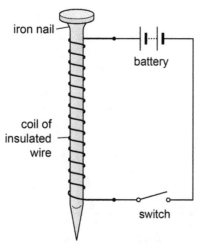

iron nail

battery

coil of
insulated
wire

switch

a.   An electromagnet can be used in a scrap yard to pick up, move around and release large metal objects, such as the bodies of cars. Explain how this works.   **[2 marks]**

_____

_____

_____

_____

b.   A scrapyard electromagnet must produce a much stronger magnetic field than the one in the circuit shown above. Suggest **two** ways that this electromagnet can be made stronger.   **[2 marks]**

1 _____

2 _____

Total marks _____ /16

Physics – Energy: work done, heating and cooling

1 Draw **one** line from each term to the correct description. [4 marks]

Term	Description
work done	Energy is transferred by hot water rising and cold water sinking, causing circulation.
conduction	Energy is transferred to an object when it is pushed along a floor.
convection	Energy is transferred by infrared waves.
radiation	Energy is transferred by particles vibrating in a solid.

2 We can make work easier by using machines, such as levers.

Complete the following sentences. Use terms from the list. You will need to use some terms more than once. You do not need to use all the terms. [5 marks]

work done   **distance moved**   **force**   **changes**

halved   **remains constant**   **doubled**

Work done = _____ × _____

The work done to move an object a given distance _____ for different lengths of lever.

A lever makes it easier to do work because it reduces the _____ needed to move an object a given distance.

If the force need is halved, the length of lever is _____.

3 The diagram shows a graph of temperature against time for a pure substance.

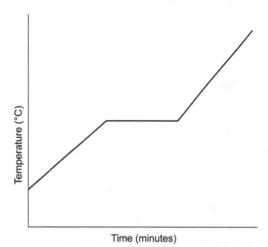

Temperature (°C)

Time (minutes)

a. This graph shows a process of physical change. Choose which process.

Tick **one** box. **[1 mark]**

A liquid cooling, then freezing to become a solid, then cooling more. ☐

A liquid warming up, then evaporating to produce gas, then warming up more. ☐

A liquid warming up, then boiling to become a gas, then warming up more. ☐

A gas cooling, then condensing to become a liquid, then cooling more. ☐

b. Look at the final sloped section of the graph. Describe what happens to the separation and motion of the particles in the substance over time. **[1 mark]**

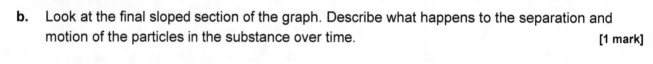

4 The diagram shows a vacuum flask.

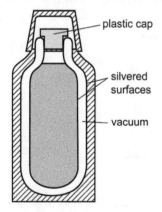

plastic cap

silvered surfaces

vacuum

The dark grey outside layer is an insulator that reduces conduction.

Explain **three** other ways that the flask keeps hot drinks hot. Remember to include a process of transferring energy for each explanation: conduction, convection, evaporation or radiation. **[3 marks]**

1 _____

2 _____

3 _____

Physics – Energy: work done, heating and cooling core

5 A freshly made cup of tea is too hot to drink at first. We leave the tea to cool until we can drink it.

   a. We can draw a conclusion from this observation.

   Choose the **best** conclusion.   **[1 mark]**

   Tick **one** box.

   Energy is transferred from a colder to a hotter place. ☐

   Energy is transferred from a hotter to a colder place. ☐

   Energy is transferred from the cup to the air by radiation. ☐

   Energy is transferred from the tea to the cup by convection. ☐

   b. This observation produces further questions we could investigate scientifically.

   Choose a suitable question we could investigate.   **[1 mark]**

   Tick **one** box.

   We could investigate:

   the rate at which the tea transfers energy by measuring its temperature
   at different times. ☐

   whether the tea transfers energy by convection by using cups made
   with different materials. ☐

   whether evaporation occurs by repeating the experiment for different
   room temperatures. ☐

   whether the tea transfers energy by radiation by blowing air over
   the surface. ☐

   Total marks _____ /16

Physics – Energy: work done, heating and cooling

1   Conduction is the transfer of energy by the vibrations of particles in a solid.

　　Define **convection** in a similar way.   [2 marks]

_____

_____

2   Some energy transfers require a medium. They can only take place when particles of a substance are present.

　　Some energy transfers can take place even when there is no medium.

　　Choose whether each of the following energy transfers needs a medium.

　　Tick **one** box for each energy transfer.   [3 marks]

Energy transfer	Medium	No medium
Conduction	☐	☐
Radiation	☐	☐
Convection	☐	☐

3   We can make work easier by using machines, such as levers.

　　　Work done = force × distance moved

　　The diagram shows a simplified diagram of a car jack.

a.   A mechanic uses a car jack to lift a weight of 5000 N by 0.20 m.

　　Calculate the work done.   [2 marks]

_____

　　Answer _____ units _____

b.   The mechanic operating the car jack applies a force of 500 N.

　　Estimate how far the mechanic has to move the handle of the car jack. Show your working.

                                                                                           [2 marks]

_____

_____

　　Answer _____ m

c. In real life, the car jack is not perfectly efficient. The energy the mechanic transfers to the car jack is greater than the work done by the car jack in lifting the car.

Suggest **two** other transfers that explain where the 'extra' energy goes. **[2 marks]**

1 _____

2 _____

4 A student investigates the rate at which a freshly made cup of tea changes temperature.

The diagram shows the apparatus he uses.

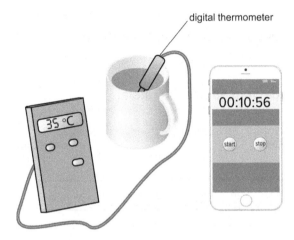

The graph shows his results.

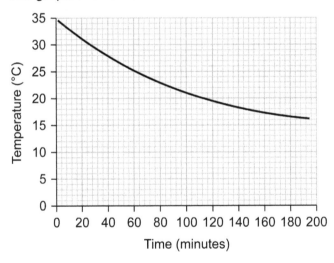

a. We can draw a conclusion from this experiment.

Choose the **best** conclusion. **[1 mark]**

Tick **one** box.

Energy is transferred from a colder to a hotter place. ☐

Energy is transferred from a hotter to a colder place. ☐

Energy is transferred from the cup to the air by radiation. ☐

Energy is transferred from the tea to the cup by convection. ☐

b. There are many different ways in which energy is transferred to and from the surroundings in this experiment.

Suggest **two** ways to change the apparatus to reduce energy transfers with the surroundings. For each change, give the method of energy transfer it reduces. **[2 marks]**

1 _____

_____

2 _____

_____

c. This experiment produces further questions the student could investigate scientifically.

An example is:

Investigate whether the material the cup is made from affects the rate at which the tea transfers energy.

Write another suitable question he could investigate. **[2 marks]**

_____

_____

Total marks _____ /16

Physics – Waves: properties and effects

1 Sound waves can be reflected. What do we call this?

Give the name. **[1 mark]**

_____

2 The table shows the properties of waves.

Type of wave	Speed of wave in air (m/s)	Transverse or longitudinal
_____	300 000 000	_____
_____	330	_____

a. Use the values for speed to complete the first column by writing 'light' or 'sound'. **[2 marks]**

b. Complete the third column by writing 'transverse' or 'longitudinal'. **[2 marks]**

3 The diagram shows a representation of the spectrum of light.

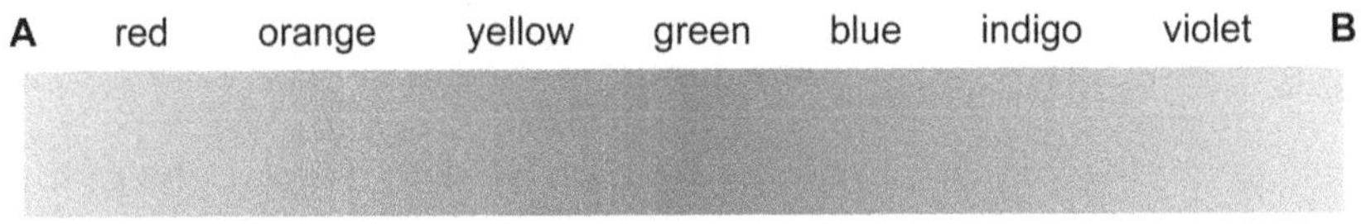

A   red   orange   yellow   green   blue   indigo   violet   B

a. Name the area **A** of the spectrum, to the left of red. **[1 mark]**

_____

b. Name the area **B** of the spectrum, to the right of violet. **[1 mark]**

_____

c. Suntan lotion blocks waves in part of this spectrum. Name the part of the spectrum. **[1 mark]**

_____

d. Explain why it is important to wear suntan lotion on sunny summer days. **[2 marks]**

_____

_____

4 The diagram shows parallel water wavefronts approaching a barrier.

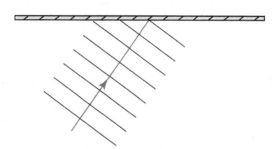

a. Describe what will happen to the wavefronts when they meet the barrier. **[1 mark]**

_____

b. Draw on the diagram to show wavefronts after they have met the barrier. **[2 marks]**

5 The diagram shows two waves that meet. Their crests coincide (they line up together).

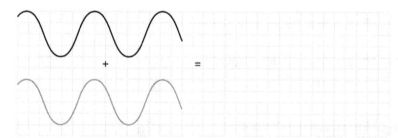

a. Complete the diagram to show the resultant wave after the two waves have added together.

[1 mark]

b. Sometimes two waves line up so the crests of one wave coincide with the troughs of the other wave.

Predict what will happen and what the resulting wave form looks like when these two waves add together. **[2 marks]**

_____

_____

Total marks _____ /16

Physics – Waves: properties and effects core

Physics – Waves: properties and effects

1 Waves are either transverse or longitudinal.

Choose whether the following waves are transverse or longitudinal.

For each wave, tick **one** box. [3 marks]

Wave	Transverse	Longitudinal
On the surface of water	☐	☐
Sound	☐	☐
Light	☐	☐

2 Describe the difference between transverse waves and longitudinal waves. [2 marks]

_____

_____

3 The diagram shows two waves that meet. Their crests coincide (they line up together).

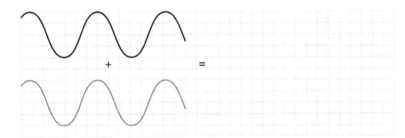

Complete the diagram to show the resultant wave after the two waves have added together. [1 mark]

4 The experimental diagram shows apparatus used to measure the speed of sound.

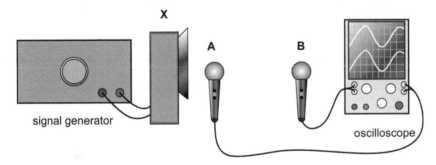

Complete the following sentences. Use terms from the list. [5 marks]

microphone   loudspeaker   distance   frequency   time

The signal generator is set to a _____ in Hz.

The _____ at **X** produces a beat of sound.

The sound wave travels past each _____, **A** and **B**.

The oscilloscope screen displays two peaks that show when the sound passed.

The _____ between the peaks tells us the _____ the sound takes to travel from **A** to **B**.

5   The apparatus from Question **4** is used to determine the speed of sound.

The diagram shows the output on an oscilloscope screen.

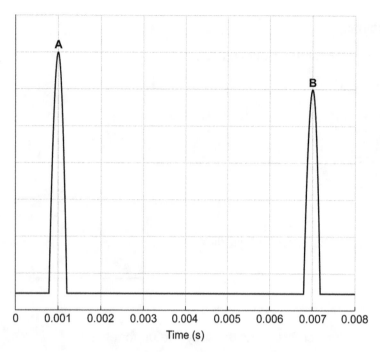

a.   Determine the time between peaks **A** and **B**.   [1 mark]

_____

b.   The distance between **A** and **B** on the apparatus is 2.0 metres.

Use your answer to part **a** and this distance to calculate the speed of sound.   [2 marks]

_____

_____

c.   Suggest **one** way you could use the apparatus to improve the accuracy of the
estimate of the speed of sound.   [2 marks]

_____

_____

Total marks _____ /16

Year 7 Baseline Test: Biology (answers)

Q	Answer	AO	Marks
1a	1 meal moth 2 blackbird	AO1	1
1b	prey	AO1	1
1c	meal moth; stick insect; blackbird *1 mark for one correct answer, 2 marks for three correct answers.*	AO2	2
1d	an organism that has a backbone	AO1	1
2a	Bar chart bars plotted accurately for tree B (1) and tree C (1)	AO2	2
2b	a ruler	AO2	1
2c	They can reproduce (1). They can grow (1).	AO2	2
2d	water	AO1	1
3	They enable the owl to capture prey (1) so they can eat and are more likely to survive (1).	AO2	2
4	heart – an organ that pumps blood around the body blood vessels – tubes that carry blood around the body blood – a liquid that transports nutrients around the body stomach – an organ that is involved in digestion	AO1	3
5	The man's heart will get stronger.	AO1	1
6a	102 bpm	AO3	1
6b	heart rate	AO2	1
6c	Exercise increases the heart rate.	AO3	1

Year 7 Baseline Test: Chemistry (answers)

Q	Answer	AO	Marks
1a	B	AO2	1
1b	The nail is magnetic (1). The stone and sand are not magnetic, so the magnet will attract the nails (1).	AO1	2
1c	D	AO1	1
1d	The sand will pass through the holes (1). The small stones are too big to pass through the holes so they will stay on the sieve (1).	AO2	2
2	Diagram correctly labelled. *From left to right:* evaporation (1); wind (1); rain (1)	AO1	3 (1 mark for each correct label)
3a	C	AO2	1
3b	A	AO3	1
3c	The white solid disappeared (1) leaving a colourless liquid (1). *Accept 'solid' disappeared.*	AO2	2
3d	Put the thermometer (B) into the beaker (1). Once the coloured liquid in the thermometer stops moving, read the temperature from the scale (1).	AO1	2
4a	*Row 2 – reversible* *Row 3 – non-reversible*	AO2	1 (both needed for 1 mark)
4b	Student A is correct (1) because the evidence shows that non-reversible changes take place when the candle burns (1).	AO2	2
4c	The flat balloon became a large, round balloon (1). A gas was made when the bicarbonate soda was mixed with the vinegar which filled/inflated the flat balloon (1).	AO3	2

Year 7 Baseline Test: Physics (answers)

Q	Answer	AO	Marks
1	**fall** (1); **mass** (1); **weight** (1); **gravity** (1)	AO1	4
2a	Weight *Accept* force due to gravity *or* gravitational force *but do not accept gravity on its own.*	AO1	1
2b	Air resistance *Accept* drag *or* friction with air	AO1	1
3a	(The) Sun	AO1	1
3b	Light from the Sun reflects off the Moon (to our eyes).	AO2	1
4	Light travels in straight lines.	AO2	1
5a	Cell *Accept* battery *or* power supply	AO1	1
5b	 *Drawn in the space on the circuit diagram, to complete the circuit.*	AO2	1
5c	Both lamps will shine less brightly than Experiment 1.	AO2	1
6	**True** (1); **True** (1); **False** (1)	AO2	3
7a	Length (of lever)	AO2	1
7b	As the lever gets longer, the force needed to move the weight gets smaller. *Accept* As the lever gets shorter, the force needed to move the weight gets larger.	AO3	1
7c	 *Three points plotted correctly* (2) *Two points plotted correctly* (1) *One or no points plotted correctly* (0)	AO2	2

Q	Answer	AO	Marks
7d	C	AO3	1

Year 8 Baseline Test: Biology (answers)

Q	Answer	AO	Marks
1a	grass	AO1	1
1b	grasshopper	AO1	1
1c	the movement of energy *Accept energy.*	AO1	1
1d	The number of grass plants would decrease (1) because there would be more grasshoppers, as there would be fewer mice to eat them (1).	AO2	2
2a	A	AO1	1
2b	red blood cells *Also accept white blood cells.*	AO1	1
2c	to hold bones together	AO2	1
3	testes – where sperm are made sperm duct – the tube that carries sperm from the testes to the urethra during ejaculation urethra – the tube that carries urine or sperm to the tip of the penis *Award one mark for one correct line and 2 marks for 3 correct lines.*	AO1	2
4	the stomach	AO2	1
5a	slide A	AO3	1
5b	Because cells on slide A contain a cell wall and chloroplasts (1), which are not found in animal cells (1).	AO2/AO3	2
6	sandbur; animal; it has spikes to stick to animals fur dandelion; wind; the seed has a parachute that catches the wind	AO2/AO3	2
7	a section of DNA that has instructions for a characteristic	AO1	1
8a	In a normal population, some people are very tall and some are very short, but most people are somewhere in between.	AO3	1
8b	continuous variation (1) Height is a characteristic that changes gradually over a range of values (1).	AO2/AO3	2

Q	Answer	AO	Marks
1a	calcium + hydrochloric acid – calcium chloride and hydrogen gas are formed calcium carbonate + hydrochloric acid – calcium chloride, water and carbon dioxide are formed calcium hydroxide + hydrochloric acid – calcium chloride and water are formed	AO2	2 (1 mark if 1 or 2 incorrect)
1b	1–2 (the pH of a strong acid)	AO1	1
1c	Neutralisation	AO1	1
1d	The pH will start around 1–2 (1). When the neutralisation reaction is complete the pH will be 7. As more calcium hydroxide is added the pH will slowly increase further to about pH 12, depending on how much alkali is added (1). *Accept an answer that describes increasing from the low pH of an acid to any pH that is alkaline.*	AO2	2
2a	plastic – non-metal aluminium – metal	AO1	1 (both needed for 1 mark)
2b	material	AO2	1
2c	*Any one of:* Volume of cube Temperature of cube	AO2	1
2d	The materials made from metal weigh more than those made from non-metals. *Accept any correct statement made from the data provided.*	AO2	1
2e	Lead is more dense than aluminium (1). The particles/atoms of lead are bigger/heavier than those of aluminium (1). *Also accept that in 1 cm^3 there are more lead particles than there are aluminium particles.*	AO3	2
3a	potassium	AO2	1
3b	A displacement reaction has taken place (1). The orange–pink solid is copper metal that has been displaced by the calcium from the blue copper sulfate solution as calcium sulfate is formed (1). Calcium sulfate solution is colourless (1). *Accept also correct word/symbol equation.*	AO3	3
4a	As the salt water is heated the water molecules begin to move more until they have enough energy to escape into the gaseous state (1). They then move into the cold condenser where they lose their energy (1) and start to	AO3	3 (for 3 marks answer must refer to particles' movement and energy)

	slow down until they return to the liquid state and collect as distilled water (1). Do not accept only the words 'evaporation' and 'condensation'.		
4b	Reduce the volume of seawater by half by heating, and then leave it in a warm place for salt crystals to form.	AO3	1

Year 8 Baseline Test: Physics (answers)

Q	Answer	AO	Marks
1	Voltmeter (1)	AO1	1
2	kinetic energy store – changes when an object speeds up gravitational potential – changes when an object is raised up energy store thermal energy store – changes when an object is warmed up elastic energy store – changes when an object is stretched or compressed *All four lines correct* (3) *Two or three lines correct* (2) *One line correct* (1)	AO1	3
3	<table><tr><th>Ammeter number</th><th>Ammeter reading, current (A)</th></tr><tr><td>1</td><td>0.8</td></tr><tr><td>2</td><td>0.4</td></tr><tr><td>3</td><td>0.4 (1)</td></tr><tr><td>4</td><td>0.8 (1)</td></tr></table>	AO2	2
4	As the comb rubs on the hair, electric charges/electrons transfer from hair to comb (1). The charges on the hair and on the comb are opposite (1) so the hair is attracted towards the comb (1).	AO2	3
5a	Gravitational potential (energy store) *Accept* potential	AO2	1
5b	Gravitational potential energy store transfers to kinetic energy store due to movement.	AO2	1
5c	Moving and accelerating	AO2	1
5d	Moving and decelerating	AO2	1

Q	Answer	AO	Marks
5e	 Line starts and goes right from end of existing curve (1) Line is curved with a gradient that decreases steadily (1) Line ends up at the horizontal (stationary) (1)	AO3	3
6a	The total energy used is not 2554 kW h (1). *Accept a description/reason such as* 'the calculation of units/kW h used is not correct' (1).	AO3	1
6b	11 018 – 07464 = 3554 (kW h) (1) 3554 × 5.5 (1) = 19 547 p = £195.47 (1) *Accept* 19 547 p for (1). *Accept errors carried forward from an incorrect subtraction.*	AO2	3

Based on a judgement of the level of demand of each test we would estimate that students who achieve 80% or more on core tests would be on track to achieve a grade 5 at GCSE level and students who achieve 80% of more on extended tests would be on track to achieve a grade 7 or above at GCSE level. Please bear in mind that progress is not always linear and that teachers remain the best judge of student performance. This is for your guidance only.

Biology – Organisms: skeletal and muscular systems (core)

Q	Answer	AO	Marks
1	To allow movement (1) To protect organs (1)	AO1	2
2	To protect the brain	AO2	1
3	bone marrow	AO1	1
4a	The arm will bend more/lower arm will move upwards.	AO2	1
4b	muscle	AO1	1
5	When running, the muscle exerts a pulling force on the bone (1). If the muscle is damaged, the athlete could find it difficult/painful to move his leg (1).	AO2	2
6	hinge – forwards and backwards ball and socket – forwards, backwards and rotation pivot – rotation around an axis	AO1	2
7	Hip or shoulder (Allow marks for any other named example of ball and socket joint.)	AO2	1
8	quadriceps – relaxes – contracts hamstring – contracts – relaxes	AO2	2
9a	57.1 N	AO3	1
9b	Week 4	AO3	1
9c	It increased then decreased	AO3	1

Biology – Organisms: skeletal and muscular systems (extended)

Q	Answer	AO	Marks
1	*Any two of:* movement protection to make red blood cells	AO1	2
2	protection	AO2	1
3	bone marrow	AO1	1
4	backwards and forwards (1) accept hip, shoulder or any other ball and socket joint (1)	AO2	2
5a	C	AO1	1
5b	D	AO1	1

6	The tendon is needed for the muscle to exert a pulling force on the bone (1). If the tendon is damaged, the athlete could find it difficult/painful to move his leg (1).	AO2	2
7	The bicep muscle relaxes and becomes longer (1). At the same time the tricep muscle contracts and shortens (1).	AO2	2
8a	Week 4	AO3	1
8b	It increased between week 1 and 4, then decreased between week 4 and 6.	AO3	1
8c	During week 5 (1) because the force measurement taken at the end of week 5 decreased significantly (1).	AO3	2

Biology – Organisms: cells to systems (core)

Q	Answer	AO	Marks
1	cell – tiny building block that living things are made from tissue – a group of cells that have a similar structure and function organ – a group of tissues that work together to carry out a function	AO1	2
2	The circulatory system	AO1	1
3a	A – the nucleus (1) B – the cell membrane (1)	AO1	2
3b	It controls the cell.	AO1	1
4a	B (cell wall)	AO2/AO3	1
4b	C (cell membrane)	AO2/AO3	1
4c	A microscope	AO2	1
5a	*Any two of:* They contain chloroplasts. They have cell walls. They contain large vacuoles.	AO3	2
5b	The stain adds colour to the structures in the cell so they are easier to see.	AO2	1
6a	Chloroplasts	AO2	1
6b	It allows the *Euglena* to swim (1), so it can move towards food/light or away from predators (1).	AO2	2
7	So the amoeba can absorb vital nutrients	AO2	1

Biology – Organisms: cells to systems (extended)

Q	Answer	AO	Marks
1	A tiny living unit	AO1	1
2	The nucleus – controls the cell (1) The cell membrane – controls what enters and leaves the cell (1)	AO1	2

3	(d) cell>tissue>organ>system	AO1	1
4	Tissues are made of similar cells that have a similar function (1), whereas organs are made from different tissues that work together to carry out a particular function (1).	AO1	2
5a	*Any two of:* They have cells walls. They contain chloroplasts. They contain large vacuoles.	AO2/AO3	2
5b	The stain adds colour to the structures in the cell so they are easier to see.	AO2	1
6	Eyepiece lens – the part you look through Stage – the flat surface where you put the slide Focusing wheel – the part you turn to produce a clear image	AO1	2
7a	It contains chloroplasts.	AO2/AO3	1
7b	The flagellum allows the *Euglena* to move/swim, (1) so that it can move towards food sources/light/move away from danger (1).	AO2	2
8	It allows vital nutrients (1) to move into the organism (1).	AO2	2

Biology – Ecosystems and habitats (core)

Q	Answer	AO	Marks
1a	grass → grasshopper → snake → hawk (All must be in correct order for mark to be awarded)	AO1	1
1b	grass	AO1	1
1c	The number of hawks would decrease (1) because if there were fewer snakes hawks would have less food (1)	AO2	2
2	The algae population will decrease (1) because there will be more tadpoles to eat the algae if there are fewer small fish to eat tadpoles (1).	AO2/AO3	2
3a	Bar drawn accurately on the chart.	AO2	1
3b	The population is decreasing.	AO3	1
3c	An increase in use of pesticides (1) A loss of habitat (1)	AO2	2
4	The number of mammee apples produced would decrease (1) because there would be fewer bees to pollinate the flowers and produce the fruit (1).	AO2	2
5a	The chemical was washed off the fields and into the pond by the rain (1). The chemical was absorbed by the algae roots in the pond (1).	AO2	2

Q	Answer	AO	Marks
5b	Algae containing DDT were eaten by small fish and then lots of small fish were eat by a few big fish (1). This resulted in DDT building up in the large fish (1).	AO2	2

Biology – Ecosystems and habitats (extended)

Q	Answer	AO	Marks
1a	habitat – the place where an organism lives population – all the members of a single species that live in a habitat environment – all the conditions that surround a living organism	AO1	2
2	energy (1); producer (1)	AO1	2
3	The snail population will increase (1) because there are no frogs to eat them/fewer predators (1).	AO2	2
4a	2.5 million	AO3	1
4b	*Any one of:* destruction of bee habitat increase in agriculture/industry increased use of pesticides disease climate change *Accept other plausible suggestions.*	AO2/AO3	1
4c	The number of mammee apples produced would decrease (1) because there would be fewer bees to pollinate the flowers and produce the fruit (1).	AO2	2
5a	Points plotted accurately	AO2	1
5b	The lynx had more food to eat as there were more snowshoe hares (1). Lynx were, therefore, more likely to survive and reproduce (1).	AO3	2
6	The plankton absorb the mercury from the ocean (1). The plankton are eaten by the small fish. Because the fish eat lots of plankton, the concentration of mercury is higher in the small fish than in the plankton (1). This process continues up the food chain so the tuna ends up with the highest concentration/the mercury builds up in the food chain (1).	AO3	3

Biology – Plant reproduction (core)

Q	Answer	AO	Marks
1a	C	AO1	1
1b	B	AO1	1
1c	A	AO1	1

2	pollen (1); seed (1)	AO1	2
3	Insects transfer pollen from the anther of one lavender flower to the stigma of another lavender flower (1) when they travel from flower to flower collecting nectar or other sources of food (1).	AO2	2
4	The ovule and pollen cell meet.	AO1	1
5	Animals eat the fruit (1). The seeds are carried in the animal/in the intestines and end up where the faeces are deposited (1).	AO2	2
6a	22	AO2	1
6b	A (1) Seed A travelled the furthest and wind pollinated plants usually have features so that they travel far in the wind (1).	AO3	2
6c	The type of seed	AO2	1
7	The results for sugar concentrations between 5 and 20 per cent support her conclusion as the number of pollen tubes increase from 2 to 15 (1), but at 25 per cent sugar the number of pollen tubes decreases to 6, which does not support her conclusion (1).	AO3	2

Biology – Plant reproduction (extended)

Q	Answer	AO	Marks
1a	A anther B stigma	AO1	2
2	Pollen is transferred from the male part of the plant/anther (1) to the female part of the plant/stigma (1).	AO1	2
3a	The paintbrush transfers pollen from the anther of one flower to the stigma of another (1). This increases the chances of pollination and, therefore, the development of a strawberry fruit (1).	AO2	2
3b	The nectar attracts insects to fly from one flower to another (1), which increases the chances of pollen transfer/ pollination (1). (Accept nectar is a food source for insects.)	AO2	2
4	Pollen cell lands on female part of plant. – 1 A pollen tube grows out of the pollen cell. – 2 The nucleus of the pollen cell meets the nucleus of an ovule. – 4 The pollen tube reaches the ovary. – 3 (All must be correct for the mark to be awarded.)	AO1	1
5	The seed will germinate further away from the parent plant (1) and so there is less competition for water/light/minerals/nutrients.(1)	AO2	2

6a	22	AO2	1
6b	A (1) Seed A travelled the furthest and wind pollinated plants usually have features so that they travel far in the wind (1).	AO3	2
7	No, it is only true for the glucose concentrations 5, 10 and 15 per cent (1). At 20 per cent the average length of the pollen tube was 71 μm which does not support her conclusion (1). *Answer must contain evidence from table*	AO3	2

Biology – Variation (core)

Q	Answer	AO	Marks
1a	*Any one of:* both have four legs both have a tail both have a mane *Accept any other similarities.*	AO2	1
1b	*Any one of:* one is taller/shorter one has longer/shorter tail one is sturdier/less study *Accept any other differences.*	AO2	1
1c	A species	AO1	1
2	Variation	AO1	1
3	continuous (1), discontinuous (1)	AO1	2
4	foot length – continuous (1) arm span – continuous (1) length of a leaf – continuous (1) fur colour – discontinuous (1)	AO2	4
5a	Graph completed with bars plotted accurately (1); bars of equal width (1)	AO2/AO3	2
5b	O	AO3	1
5c	Their genes	AO1	1
6	There are only 14 in the class which is a small sample and therefore not reliable/representative of the population (1). Class results are 71% unattached ear lobes, whereas the population is 99% (1).	AO2/AO3	2

Biology – Variation (extended)

Q	Answer	AO	Marks
1a	*Any one of:*	AO2	1

	all have four legs		
	all have a tail		
	all have fur		
	(Accept any other similarities.)		
1b	*Any one of:*	AO2	1
	it has tusks		
	it has a trunk		
	it has large ears		
	(Accept any other differences.)		
2	A group of organisms with similar characteristics that reproduce together to give fertile offspring	AO1	1
3	The differences in characteristics found within a species	AO1	1
4	continuous (1), discontinuous (1)	AO1	2
5	Foot length – continuous (1)	AO2	3
	Arm span – continuous (1)		
	Length of femur bone – continuous (1)		
6a	Graph completed with: variables on correct axis and clearly labelled, (1) appropriate scale (1) and bars plotted accurately (1).	AO2/AO3	3
6b	A and O	AO3	1
	(Both needed for the mark.)		
6d	Their genes	AO2	1
7	There are only 14 in the class which is a small sample and therefore not reliable/representative of the population (1). Class results are 71% unattached ear lobes, whereas the population in 99% (1).	AO2/AO3	2

Biology – Human reproduction (core)

Q	Answer	AO	Marks
1a	uterus	AO1	1
1b	ovary	AO1	1
1c	A	AO1	1
2	ovulation – the release of eggs	AO1	2
	fertilisation – the joining of the nucleus of an egg and a sperm cell		
	gestation – the period of development of a foetus from fertilised egg to birth		
	(1 mark for one correct line, 2 marks for all three lines correct.)		
3	gamete	AO1	1
4	To make sperm	AO1	1
	(Also accept to produce hormones.)		
5a	Day 4	AO3	1

5b	Day 14				AO2/AO3	1
6	**Substance**	**Passes from mother's blood to foetus' blood**	**Passes from foetus' blood to mother's blood**		AO1	3 (1 mark for each correct row)
	oxygen	✓				
	carbon dioxide		✓			
	glucose	✓				
7	Alcohol can move from the mother's blood into the foetus' blood (1) and can harm the foetus/cause stillbirth/lower birth weight (1). (Accept other risks.)				AO2	2
8a	3500 – 3255 = 245 g				AO2	1
8b	The more cigarettes smoked by a mother, the lower the average birthweight of the baby.				AO3	1

Biology – Human reproduction (extended)

Q	Answer	AO	Marks
1a	ovary	AO1	1
1b	To store/release eggs	AO1	1
1c	Oviduct labelled correctly (tube connecting ovary and uterus)	AO1	1
2	gamete	AO1	1
3	Ovulation is the release of an egg from an ovary (1). Fertilisation is the fusing of the nuclei of an egg and a sperm cell (1).	AO1	2
4	35–36 °C	AO2	1
5a	Day 4	AO3	1
5b	Day 14	AO3	1
5c	It is ready to receive a fertilised egg.	AO3	1
6	gestation	AO1	1

7	**Substance**	**Passes from mother's blood to foetus' blood**	**Passes from foetus' blood to mother's blood**	**Does not pass between mother's blood and foetus' blood**	AO1	3 (1 mark for each correct row)
	oxygen	✓				
	carbon dioxide		✓			
	glucose	✓				

8	Large-scale studies have shown that babies of mothers who smoked in pregnancy are about 150–200 g lighter at birth (1). A study of 4500 mothers found that smokers had a 40% higher risk of premature birth compared with non-smokers (1).	AO3	2

Based on a judgement of the level of demand of each test we would estimate that students who achieve 80% or more on core tests would be on track to achieve a grade 5 at GCSE level and students who achieve 80% of more on extended tests would be on track to achieve a grade 7 or above at GCSE level. Please bear in mind that progress is not always linear and that teachers remain the best judge of student performance. This is for your guidance only.

Chemistry – The particulate nature of matter (core)

Q	Answer	AO	Marks
1a	*From left to right:* liquid (1); gas (1); solid (1)	AO1	3
1b	In the cup the particles are in fixed, regular positions (1) but in the milk the particles are in random positions and can move around (1).	AO3	2
1c	There are spaces between the particles in a gas but the particles in a solid or liquid are touching (1). Therefore the particles in a gas can be pushed together easily but those in a solid or liquid cannot (1).	AO3	2
2	subliming – solid to gas condensing – gas to liquid evaporating – liquid to gas freezing – liquid to solid	AO1	3 (3 marks if all correct, 2 marks if 3 correct, 1 mark if 1 or 2 correct)
3a	The solid ice cube (1) seen at the start gradually got smaller until it disappeared (1).	AO3	2
3b	Diagram should show particles loosely arranged, as in a liquid.	AO2	1
4a	diffusion	AO3	1
4b	The 'bread' particles move from an area of high concentration inside the shop to an area of low concentration outside the shop.	AO3	1
4c	The smell of bread will get fainter until they can no longer smell it.	AO3	1

Chemistry – The particulate nature of matter (extended)

Q	Answer	AO	Marks
1a	*Any one of:* Diamond is a solid at room temperature but golden syrup is a liquid. Diamond is hard whereas golden syrup is soft. Diamond has a fixed shape whereas golden syrup is runny. Diamond is strong whereas golden syrup is weak. *Or other suitable answer.*	AO1	1
1b	Particles are in fixed, regular positions.	AO2	1
1c	Golden syrup is a liquid (1). The particles in a liquid move randomly and have no fixed positions (1).	AO3	2

1d	Gas pressure is caused by the particles colliding with the walls of the can (1). As the deodorant is used up there are fewer particles in the can, so there are fewer collisions with the wall of the can, therefore the gas pressure decreases (1).	AO3	2
2a	*Top label* – sublimation (1) *Lower label* – freezing (1)	AO1	2
3a	diffusion	AO3	1
3b	The 'bread' particles move from an area of high concentration inside the shop to an area of low concentration outside the shop.	AO3	1
3c	The smell of bread will get fainter until they can no longer smell it.	AO3	1
4a	*Any one of:* water ethanol mercury	AO2	1
4b	*Any one of:* tin salt	AO2	1
4c	A substance is a gas at any temperature above its boiling point (1). 20°C is a higher temperature than the boiling point of helium which is –268°C (1).	AO2	2
4d	It takes more energy to break the forces between the particles in salt than those in tin.	AO3	1

Chemistry – Pure and impure substances (core)

Q	Answer	AO	Marks
1a	pure (1); one (1); two (1); chemically (1)	AO1	4
1b	milk	AO1	1
1c	It contains different types of particles.	AO2	1
2a	*Diagram 1* – distillation (1) *Diagram 2* – chromatography (1) *Diagram 3* – filtration (1)	AO1	3
2b	Distillation (1). It is a mixture of two liquids with different boiling points (1).	AO2	2
3a	1 dissolving 2 filtering 3 evaporating 4 crystallising	AO2	3 (3 marks for all in correct order, 2 marks if 2 correct)
3b	The filter stops the solid (1) while letting the liquid pass through the small holes (1).	AO2	2

Chemistry – Pure and impure substances (extended)

Q	Answer	AO	Marks
1a	Temperature	AO2	1
1b	Solubility *or* mass of potassium nitrate dissolving in 100 g of water.	AO2	1
1c	*Any one of:* Volume of water Size of potassium nitrate crystal Speed/duration of stirring	AO2	1
1d	Solid left in the bottom of the tube.	AO2	1
1e	As the temperature increases so does the solubility.	AO2	1
1f	Water molecules move in between the particles of potassium nitrate (1) as they break the forces of attraction between them (1).	AO3	2
2a	3	AO2	1
2b	A black spot is in the same position on all of the chromatograms.	AO2	1
2c	As the water moves up the paper it takes the dissolved dye with it (1). The different substances then travel different distances up the paper (1).	AO2	2
3a	*Top:* condenser (1) *Bottom:* distilled water (1)	AO1	2
3b	As the salt water is heated the water molecules begin to move more until they have enough energy to escape into the gaseous state (1). They then move into the cold condenser where they lose their energy to their surroundings (1) and start to slow down until they return to the liquid state (1). *Do not accept only the words 'evaporation' and 'condensation'.*	AO3	3 (for 3 marks answer must refer to particles' movement and energy)

Chemistry – Acids and alkalis (core)

Q	Answer	AO	Marks
1a	indicator – is used to identify whether a solution is acidic or alkaline (1) base – a substance that neutralises an acid (1) acid – has pH below 7 (1)	AO1	3
1b	First and fourth hazard symbols	AO2	1 (both must be correct for 1 mark)
1c	*Any one of:* Wear safety glasses/goggles Wear gloves	AO1	1
1d	Hydrogen	AO1	1

2a	Diagram correctly labelled.	AO1	3
	From left to right: Increasingly acidic (1); Neutral (1); Increasingly alkaline (1)		
2b	Hand soap is a weak alkali (1).	AO2	2
	Oven cleaner is a strong alkali (1).		
2c	Red cabbage indicator will only tell you if a sample is acidic or alkaline (1) but universal indicator will tell you how acidic or alkaline a sample is (1).	AO2	2
3a	3	AO2	1
3b	The alkali in the wasp sting is an irritant (1). When the vinegar was added, the alkali was neutralised so it was no longer an irritant (1).	AO3	2

Chemistry – Acid and alkalis (extended)

Q	Answer	AO	Marks
1a	neutralisation	AO1	1
1b	sodium chloride + water	AO1	1 (both parts must be correct for mark)
1c	Data points plotted correctly.	AO2	2 (1 mark if 2 wrongly plotted)
1d	Smooth line drawn.	AO2	1
1e	Graph line starts off flat at pH 1, rises steeply to pH 8–9, then flattens off again at pH 9.5.	AO2	2 (2 marks for details of pH, 1 mark only for general answer)
1f	The reaction is complete and this is the pH of the alkali (sodium hydroxide).	AO3	1
2	magnesium + hydrochloric acid – a chloride and hydrogen gas are formed	AO2	2 (2 marks for all correct, 1 mark if 1 or 2 correct)
	copper + sulfuric acid – no reaction		
	potassium hydroxide + hydrochloric acid – a chloride and water are formed		
3a	*Any one of:*	AO3	1
	Volume of solution		
	Temperature of solution		
	Mass of egg shell		
	Size of egg shell pieces		
3b	To act as a control; distilled water is neutral and has no sugar or acid in it.	AO2	1
3c	So they knew which solutions were acidic.	AO2	1
3d	The egg shell reacted with all the acidic solutions (1) but did not react with the sugar solution (1). Therefore the correct hypothesis is 'Acid causes tooth decay' (1).	AO3	3

Chemistry – Chemical reactions of metals and non-metals (core)

Q	Answer	AO	Marks
1a	*Reasonable answers include:* A metal spoon will be shiny but a plastic one might not (1). A metal spoon conducts heat/electricity but a plastic one does not (1). A metal spoon is malleable/bendy but the plastic one is brittle/breaks easily (1). *Or other suitable answer.*	AO1	3
1b	Plastic handles will stop you from getting burnt because they are good insulators of heat.	AO2	1
2	oxidation (1); oxygen (1); gas (1)	AO1	3
3a	oxygen	AO1	1
3b	oxygen (1); copper oxide (1)	AO1	2
3c	The particles have combined in different ways to make a new substance.	AO1	1
4a	magnesium, zinc, cobalt, copper	AO3	1
4b	The more reactive a metal is, the more bubbles will be produced.	AO2	1
4c	magnesium sulfate (1) + hydrogen (1)	AO2	2
4d	The metals will react in a similar way to their reactions with sulfuric acid.	AO3	1

Chemistry – Chemical reactions of metals and non-metals (extended)

Q	Answer	AO	Marks
1a	The grey iron filings moved towards the magnet leaving the yellow sulfur behind (1). Iron is magnetic but sulfur is not (1).	AO1	2
1b	A black solid was formed.	AO2	1
2a	The grey shiny nail is now an orange–brown colour (1). The blue solution is now a green–blue colour (1).	AO1	2
2b	Copper	AO1	1
2c	Diagram correctly drawn with black circle joined to grey circle.	AO2	1
2d	Displacement	AO1	1
2e	No changes/no reaction (1). Copper metal is less reactive than iron so cannot displace it from the solution (1).	AO3	2
2f	zinc (1) and lead (1)	AO2	2
3a	A chemical change has taken place/a new chemical substance (with a different colour) has been made.	AO2	1
3b	–3.4 g/decrease of 3.4 g *(Must indicate mass has decreased.)*	AO1	1

3c	A gas/carbon dioxide was formed.	AO3	1
3d	Mass will decrease	AO2	1

Chemistry – Earth and rocks (core)

Q	Answer	AO	Marks
1a	Diagram correctly labelled. *From top:* core (1); mantle (1); crust (1)	AO1	3
1b	igneous rock – formed from cooling magma above or below the surface metamorphic rock – formed by intense heat and pressure on other rocks sedimentary rock – formed from layers of sediment, often contains fossils	AO2	2 (2 marks if all 3 correct, 1 mark if 1 or 2 correct)
2a	Diorite has large crystals whereas dacite has small crystals.	AO3	1
2b	Large crystals are formed when magma cools down slowly (1). Small crystals are formed when magma cools down quickly (1).	AO2	2
2c	Dacite is very hard (1) because of the interlocking crystal structure found in the igneous rock (1).	AO3	2
3a	When the rocks were formed dead animals and plants were covered in layers of sediment (1). As the sediment layers cemented together over millions of years to form sandstone rock, the dead organisms were preserved as fossils within the layers (1).	AO1	2
3b	The limestone rock has weathered more than the marble rock (1). Sedimentary rocks weather more easily than metamorphic rocks because the forces between the particles in them are much weaker than those in the metamorphic rocks (1).	AO3	2
3c	Slate is a metamorphic rock (1). The forces between the particles in metamorphic rock are very strong, making it strong and resistant to weather (1).	AO3	2

Chemistry – Earth and rocks (extended)

Q	Answer	AO	Marks
1a	The plates are floating on the mantle, which is a liquid/semi-liquid.	AO2	1
1b	*Any one of:* Mountains could form. An earthquake could happen. A volcano could erupt.	AO1	1

1c	They monitor/measure the waves made by earthquakes and explosions as they travel through the Earth (1). Waves travel at different speeds in different materials (1).	AO3	2
2a	*Any two of:* weathering erosion large Earth movements (e.g. earthquakes, volcanic eruptions)	AO1	2
2b	Erosion is the movement of rock by water, ice or wind (1), whereas weathering is the wearing down of rock by physical, chemical or biological processes (1).	AO2	2
2c	*Any reasonable point with supporting science, such as:* It may have extreme temperatures, being very hot during the day and very cold at the night (1). The constant change in temperature shatters the rocks (1). It might be very cold, wet and windy (1), which are conditions for weathering of the rocks (1). The atmosphere might be acidic (1) so there is chemical weathering of the rocks (1).	AO3	2
3a	Limestone is a sedimentary rock (1). Heat and pressure cause the sedimentary rock to change into metamorphic rock before it melts and flows into the magma (1). When the pressure gets too high there is a volcanic eruption and the magma flows out of the volcano (1). As the magma cools, igneous rocks such as granite are formed in the mountains (1).	AO2	4
3b	Difference: the processes in the rock cycle are very slow whereas a chemical reaction such as burning is very fast (1). Similarity: mass is always conserved. No new particles are made or destroyed (1). *Accept other suitable answers.*	AO3	2

Chemistry – Dalton's atomic theory (core)

Q	Answer	AO	Marks
1	particles (1); atoms (1); experiments (1); calculations (1) *(experiments and calculations can be in opposite order)*	AO1	4
2a	second symbol and CO_2	AO1	2
2b	A	AO1	1
2c	Diagram drawn correctly, with black/filled circle joined to open circle (1). The atoms rearrange/combine (1).	AO2	2

3	Diagram 1 – carbon dioxide Diagram 2 – hydrogen sulfide Diagram 3 – nitrogen oxide Diagram 4 – water	AO3	3 (3 marks if all correct; 2 marks if 2 correct, 1 mark if 1 correct)
4a	The atoms rearrange (1). The oxygen atom breaks away from the copper atom, leaving it alone, and joins the magnesium atom (1).	AO2	2
4b	Mass of reactants = 2.4 + 8.0 = 10.4 g (1) Mass of products = 10.4 g Mass of copper oxide = 10.4 − 4.0 = 6.4 g (1)	AO2	2

Chemistry – Dalton's atomic theory (extended)

Q	Answer	AO	Marks
1a	Technology was not good enough to carry out the required experiments until the early 19th century.	AO2	1
1b	Subatomic particles are found in the centre of an atom (1). Atoms of different elements are the same (1).	AO1	2
1c	compound	AO1	1
2a	**B**	AO2	1
2b	**D**	AO2	1
2c	**A** or **C**	AO2	1
3a	19 mass units	AO1	1
3b	Atoms are indestructible and they rearrange during a reaction (1). So the total mass cannot change during a reaction (1). Therefore the mass of the products must equal the mass of the reactants, 1 + 19 = 20 g (1).	AO2	3
3c	18 mass units	AO2	1
3d	Total mass cannot change during the reaction (1). Mass of products = mass of reactants = 16 + (2 × 1) = 18 (1).	AO2	2
3e	Diagram drawn correctly, with 2 small/grey circles joined to large/black circle on opposite sides (1). *(Accept different order of atoms in molecule as long as they are touching.)* 12 + 32 = 44 g (1) *(Answer must include g units.)*	AO3	2

Based on a judgement of the level of demand of each test we would estimate that students who achieve 80% or more on core tests would be on track to achieve a grade 5 at GCSE level and students who achieve 80% of more on extended tests would be on track to achieve a grade 7 or above at GCSE level. Please bear in mind that progress is not always linear and that teachers remain the best judge of student performance. This is for your guidance only.

Physics – Movement: speed and acceleration (core)

Q	Answer	AO	Marks
1	average speed = $\dfrac{\text{distance travelled}}{\text{time taken}}$	AO1	1
2	kilometres per hour (1), metres per second (1)	AO1	2
3a	average speed = $\dfrac{\text{distance travelled}}{\text{time taken}} = \dfrac{6}{2} = 3$ (1) m/s *or* metres per second (1)	AO2	2
3b	The speed decreases/reduces *Accept* It slows down.	AO2	1
4	C (1); B (1); A (1)	AO2	3
5a	A	AO2	1
5b	C	AO2	1
6	The student works out the average speed (1). The cyclist sees the (instantaneous) speed at one particular time (1).	AO3	2
7a	**B** travels in the opposite direction to **A** (1) at a slower speed (1). *Accept* **B** travels the same distance as **A** but takes longer *or* **B** travels the same distance as **A** at a lower average speed.	AO2	2
7b	1.0 km	AO3	1

Physics – Movement: speed and acceleration (extended)

Q	Answer	AO	Marks
1	average speed = $\dfrac{\text{distance travelled (1)}}{\text{time taken (1)}}$	AO1	2
2a	less than 40 km/h.	AO3	1
2b	The average speed is the total distance travelled divided by the total time taken. The bus has to stop sometimes at the bus stops, so the speed is	AO2	1

Part 1 Physics *P*

	reduced to 0 km/h at these times, so the average speed is reduced.			
3a	average speed = $\dfrac{\text{distance}}{\text{time}} = \dfrac{6}{2} = 3$ (1) m/s *or* metres per second (1)	AO1/ AO2	2
3b	The speed decreases/reduces *Accept* It slows down.	AO1	1
4a i	A	AO1	1
4a ii	average speed = $\dfrac{\text{distance}}{\text{time}} = \dfrac{300}{60}$ (1) = 5 (1) m/s	AO2	2
4b i	B	AO1	1
4b ii	average speed = $\dfrac{\text{distance}}{\text{time}} = \dfrac{400}{60}$ (1) = 6.7 (1) m/s	AO2	2
5a	*One mark for straight line (shown as the dashed line here), one mark for showing correct start and end points.*	AO3	2
5b	1.0 km	AO3	1

Physics – Forces and gravity (core)

Q	Answer	AO	Marks
1	**kilograms** (1) (*accept* kg, grams, g) **newtons** (1) (*accept* N but not n) **newtons** (1) (*accept* N but not n)	AO1	3
2	**force** (1); **mass** (1); **non-contact** (1)	AO1	3

3a		AO1	1
3b	$W = mg = 20 \times 3.5$ (1) $= 70$ N (1)	AO2	2

4				AO2	3

	Mass of object (kg)	Weight of object (N)
On Earth	10	100
On Mercury	Same as (½) on Earth	Less than (1) on Earth
On Jupiter	Same as (½) on Earth	More than (1) on Earth

5a	The downwards shape/negative gradient of the line shows the ball is falling towards the ground/height is reducing (1). The downwards curve shows the ball is accelerating/speeding up as it falls (1).	AO2	2
5b	Horizontal line (1) along the x-axis (distance = 0) from 5 seconds to 8 seconds (1).	AO3	2

Physics – Forces and gravity (extended)

Q	Answer	AO	Marks
1	weight = mass (of object) × gravitational field strength *Also accept equation in symbols $W = mg$ or $W = m \times g$*	AO1	1
2a		AO1	1
2b	The force on **A** is the same size as the force on **B** (1). The direction of the force on **A** is opposite to the direction of the force on **B**/pointing to (the centre of) **B** (1).	AO2	2

3a		Gravitational field strength (N/kg)	Mass of object (kg)	Weight of object (N)	AO2	3
	On Earth	10	10	100		
	On Mercury	3.7	**10** (½)	**37** (1)		
	On Jupiter	**24.8** (1)	**10** (½)	248		

3b	Jupiter has a much larger mass than Earth (to produce a much greater gravitational field strength).	AO3	1
4a	(Instantaneous) speed *Accept* velocity	AO1	1
4b	The downwards curve shows the ball is accelerating as it falls.	AO2	1
4c	The graph will be the same (1). This is because the acceleration (due to gravity) is the same for both sizes of object/both masses (1).	AO2	2
5a	The gravitational field strength reduces as the space probe travels further away (1) until eventually it goes to zero/is very small/is negligible (1).	AO3	2
5b	The gravitational field strength of Pluto will be about 1/500 that of Earth (1). This is because the gravitational field strength of an object/a planet depends on its mass (1).	AO3	2

Physics – Electric circuits: current, potential difference and resistance (core)

Q	Answer		AO	Marks
1	**Description**	**Quantity**	AO1	3
	Opposition to the flow of charge, measured in ohms, Ω	**resistance** (1)		
	The flow of charge, measured in amperes, A	**current** (1)		
	The amount of energy transferred from a battery to the movement of charge, measured in volts, V	**potential difference** (1)		
2	—⊣⊢— cell —⊗— lamp —Ⓐ— ammeter		AO1	4

	⊣☐⊢ resistor *One mark for each correct pair.*		
3a	Series	AO1/ AO2	1
3b	*Any two of:* A parallel circuit has more than one separate branch connecting components to a cell/battery. The full potential difference (voltage) is supplied to each branch. The current is divided between the branches.	AO1/ AO2	2
4a	Switch	AO1	1
4b	*Any two of:* Add more cells/batteries. Change the bulb for one that is more energy efficient (so less energy is wasted as heat/more energy is used to produce light). Change the bulb for an LED/light-emitting diode. Remove the resistor from the circuit.	AO3	2
5a	15 mA	AO3	1
5b	*Accept any diagram that shows a complete circuit with two resistors connected in series with a cell and an ammeter.*	AO2	1
5c	7.5 mA	AO3	1

Physics – Electric circuits: current, potential difference and resistance (extended)

Q	Answer	AO	Marks
1a	Lamp *Accept* bulb	AO1	1
1b	Voltmeter	AO1	1
1c	Resistor	AO1	1
1d	Cell *Do not accept* battery *or* power supply	AO1	1
2a	Series	AO1/AO2	1
2b	*Any **two** of:*	AO1/AO2	2

	A circuit has more than one separate branch connecting components to a cell/battery. The full potential difference (voltage) is supplied to each branch. The current is divided between the branches.		
3a	Circuit **A** (parallel) has the same potential difference as the battery across each loop/branch of the circuit (1). Circuit **B** (series) shares the potential difference of the battery across both lamps, reducing the amount of energy transferred in each lamp, making them dimmer (1).	AO2	2
3b	Twice as much energy (per second) is being used in circuit **A** compared to circuit **B** (1). The battery stores a limited amount of energy, so it will run out twice as quickly in circuit **A** compared to circuit B (1).	AO3	2
4a	PVC plastic	AO2	1
4b	Variable resistor (1). Changing the resistance of the resistor changes the potential difference across the lights, so the brightness of the lights can be changed (1).	AO2	2
4c	Copper is a good conductor because it has very low resistance, PVC plastic is a good insulator because it has very high resistance (1). The high resistance stops current from flowing from the wire to a person holding the cable (1).	AO3	2

Physics – Static electricity (core)

Q	Answer	AO	Marks
1	**non-contact** (1); **contact** (1); **non-contact** (1)	AO1	3
2	**friction** (1); **electrons** (1); **positively** (1); **negatively** (1); **attract** (1)	AO1/ AO2	5
3	 *One mark for each correctly added charge sign (2).*	AO2	2
4a	The insulating material rubs against the inside of the dome/globe and rubs off electrons because of friction (1). The removal of electrons causes a positive charge to build up on the dome/globe (1). *Also accept a description that suggests electrons are deposited onto the globe; although this is not correct, it does demonstrate*	AO2	2

	that the student understands the role of friction and the movement of charge.		
4b	*Any **one** of:* Do not touch the generator before it has been discharged (to prevent shocks). Wearing insulated shoes (to prevent earthing/conduction of electricity). Wearing safety goggles in case of sparks. Wearing protective clothing/a lab coat in case of sparks. Keeping other metal and electrical devices well away from the experiment. *Also accept any other sensible safety precaution for 1 mark.*	AO3	1
5	The charge build-up causes an electric field to form between the clouds and the buildings on the ground (1). Sometimes a connection is formed between a cloud and a building, so a large electric current/lightning strike passes through the building (1). A metal rod or wire conducts the electricity to the ground and prevents damage to the building/the people inside (1).	AO3	3

Physics– Static electricity (extended)

Q	Answer	AO	Marks
1a	*Any one of:* A force that is caused by a field A force that acts at a distance A force that arises (on an object) even though nothing is touching it	AO1	1
1b	Electrons	AO1	1
2a	The sign/polarity of electrical charge (*or* plus and minus charge). Amount of charge *is not correct. There must be a reference to the sign or polarity.*	AO1	1
2b	<table><tr><td></td><td colspan="2">**Rod 1**</td></tr><tr><td>**Rod 2**</td><td>**Plastic**</td><td>**Perspex**</td></tr><tr><td>**Plastic**</td><td>Repel (1)</td><td>Attract</td></tr><tr><td>**Perspex**</td><td>Attract (1)</td><td>Repel (1)</td></tr></table>	AO1/AO2	3
3a	The insulating material rubs against the inside of the dome/globe and rubs off electrons because of friction (1). The removal of electrons causes a positive charge to build up on the dome/globe (1). *Also accept a description that suggests electrons are deposited onto the globe; although this is not correct, it does demonstrate*	AO2	2

		AO	Marks
	that the student understands the role of friction and the movement of charge.		
3b	*Any **one** of* Do not touch the generator before it has been discharged (to prevent shocks). Wearing insulated shoes (to prevent earthing/conduction of electricity). Wearing safety goggles in case of sparks. Wearing protective clothing/a lab coat in case of sparks. Keeping other metal and electrical devices well away from the experiment. *Also accept any other sensible safety precaution for 1 mark.*	AO3	1
4	Air is not a good conductor but can still transfer some electrons, so charged objects will gradually lose their charge (1). Water is a better conductor than air (1). Water vapour in the air causes charged objects to lose their charge more quickly (1).	AO2	3
5a	The electric charge in the object causes charge of the same sign/polarity to move down to the bottom of the metal rod (1). The metal rod and the gold leaf have the same sign/polarity of charge, so the gold leaf is repelled and moves upwards (1).	AO3	2
5b	The student connects the metal rod to earth so the (excess) charge flows through the student to earth (1), leaving the metal rod and gold leaf with no (net) charge, so they do not repel and the leaf drops down (1).	AO3	2

Physics – Energy: stores, transfers, power and costs (core)

Q	Answer	AO	Marks
1	chemical energy store – gas that is burned to heat a saucepan thermal energy store – a saucepan full of hot water elastic energy store – a stretched spring	AO1	3
2a	Kilowatt-hour	AO1	1

2b	Month	Final meter reading (kW h)	Initial meter reading (kW h)	Amount of energy used (kW h)	AO2	2
	March	12 675	12 549	126 (1)		
	April	12 807	12 675	132 (1)		

| 2c | Total energy used = 126 + 132 = 258 kW h (1)
 Cost = 258 × 5.7 = 1471 pence (or £14.71) (1)
 Also accept 1470 pence or £14.70) | AO2 | 2 |

3a	chemical energy store → **electrical** energy store (1)	AO2	1
3b	Lamp produces light (1). Lamp heats up/heats surroundings (1). *Accept* lamp makes a sound/buzzing noise (1).	AO2	2
3c	Total energy stored stays the same.	AO2	1
4a	Milk chocolate	AO2	1
4b	*Any one of*: Human body gives out heat all the time. We make movements (that are not all useful) all the time even when sitting still. *Any other reasonable suggestion*	AO2	1
5	**Stage 4** Change in potential energy of lifted object (1). The predicted values suggest more energy is stored by the lifted object than is available from the kinetic energy + work done, and energy must be conserved/total energy must stay the same (1).	AO3	2

Physics – Energy: stores, transfers, power and costs (extended)

Q	Answer	AO	Marks
1	**potential** (1); **transfers** (1); **kinetic** (1); **total** (1)	AO1	4
2a	Total energy into diagram/at left of diagram = total energy out of diagram/at right of diagram	AO2	1
2b	Useful energy = 100 – 25 = 75 J	AO2	1
2c	Electrical energy is transferred by heating to the thermal energy store of the surroundings.	AO2	1
3a	**C**	AO2	1
3b	*Any **two** of*: Movement of spring back to its unstretched shape transfers kinetic energy (of spring) (1). Heat/thermal energy of the spring/dissipated to the surroundings (1). Sound produced as the spring snaps back into shape (which is dissipated to the thermal energy store of the surroundings) (1).	AO2	2
4a	Milk chocolate stored the most energy per 100 g. **True** (1) A diet containing only milk chocolate is best. **Cannot tell** (1) The foods cannot be compared because the portion sizes were different. **False** (1)	AO3	3
4b	Insulating material can be used to reduce the amount of energy wasted to the surroundings as heat.	AO2	1
5	*Any **two** of*:	AO2	2

	Relying on one type of fuel/energy source is risky/might run out/might not suit all types of energy consumption (1). Burning gas produces carbon dioxide, a gas that increases global warming/climate change (1). *Any other sensible reason* (1).		

Physics – The Earth in space (core)

Q	Answer	AO	Marks
1	planet, star, galaxy, Universe	AO1	1
2a	The Earth rotates on its axis. When half of the Earth receives sunlight (day), the other half is in shade (night).	AO1	1
2b	South America and Great Britain are on opposite sides of the world – when South America is facing the Sun, Great Britain is facing away from the Sun.	AO2	1
2c	*Left-hand box* – summer in the UK *Right-hand box* – winter in the UK	AO1	2
2d	**northern** (1); **towards** (1); **winter** (1)	AO2	3
2e	0 hours	AO2	1
3a	The Earth was at the centre (1), with planets, the Sun and stars orbiting the Earth (1).	AO2/ AO3	2
3b	There was no real evidence supporting Copernicus' theory.	AO2/ AO3	1
3c	Observations of the Moon and other planets using his telescope.	AO2	1
3d	The Catholic Church believed that God was at the centre of the Universe and so Galileo's theory was considered blasphemy (irreligious).	AO3	1
3e	Other astronomers collected evidence using more accurate telescopes (1). All the evidence agreed with and supported Galileo's model (1).	AO2/ AO3	2

Physics – The Earth in space (extended)

Q	Answer	AO	Marks
1a	16 hours of daylight in Northern France compared to 24 in the Arctic circle.	AO1	1
1b	The Earth is tilted as it rotates on its axis (1) and so in summer the northern hemisphere of the Earth is tilted towards the Sun and in winter it is tilted away from it (1).	AO1	2
2a	Light years	AO1	1
2b	The distances are too great/big	AO1	1
2c	Earth to Sun is 0.000016 light years Earth to Pluto 0.00044 light years	AO2	1

	So Pluto is 27.5 times further away from the Sun than the Earth.		
2d	A light year is a measure of how far the light can travel in a year (1). The light we observed is measured from the point at which it leaves the light source, i.e. the star (1). Sirius is much closer to the Earth than the Milky Way, so the light we see from Sirius is much younger than that observed from the Milky Way (1).	AO2/ AO3	3
3a	New Moon *on the left* Last quarter Moon *at the top* *Both needed for 1 mark*	AO1	1
3b	The same half of the Moon always faces the Earth. Half the Moon is lit by reflecting the light from the Sun, and the other half is in darkness (1). The Moon orbits the Earth every 29.5 days. Therefore, the angle of the Moon that reflects the Sun's light and is seen from Earth changes throughout the month, giving the different phases of the Moon (1).	AO2	2
3c	It reflects the sunlight.	AO3	1
4a	At first it was just a theory with little supporting evidence to suggest that existing ideas were wrong. The Catholic Church strongly believed that the Earth was at the centre of the Universe. It was not until other astronomers collected evidence using more accurate telescopes that the theory was finally accepted.	AO2	3

Based on a judgement of the level of demand of each test we would estimate that students who achieve 80% or more on core tests would be on track to achieve a grade 5 at GCSE level and students who achieve 80% of more on extended tests would be on track to achieve a grade 7 or above at GCSE level. Please bear in mind that progress is not always linear and that teachers remain the best judge of student performance. This is for your guidance only.

Biology – Breathing and gas exchange (core)

Q	Answer	AO	Marks
1	A	AO1	1
1b	B	AO1	1
2	outwards (1); increases (1)	AO1	2
3a	carbon dioxide	AO2	1
3b	oxygen	AO2	1
3c	a large surface area (1) a good blood supply (1)	AO1	2
3d	It reduces the surface area of the alveoli (1) and therefore reduces the efficiency of gas exchange (1).	AO1	2
4a	lungs	AO2	1
4b	diaphragm	AO2	1
4c	It increases the volume (1) inside the bell jar so the air pressure decreases (1) causing the balloon to expand (Accept air moves into the balloon to fill the extra volume.)	AO2/AO3	2
5a	As height increases so does lung volume. (Accept reference to positive correlation.)	AO3	1
5b	180 cm	AO3	1

Biology – Breathing and gas exchange (extended)

Q	Answer	AO	Marks
1a	trachea	AO1	1
1b	bronchus	AO1	1
2a	carbon dioxide	AO1	1
2b	oxygen	AO1	1
2c	There is more oxygen in the alveoli than in the capillaries, so oxygen moves from the alveoli into the capillaries (1). There is more carbon dioxide in the capillaries than in the alveoli so blood moves from the capillaries into the alveoli (1).	AO1/AO2	2
2d	It makes the walls very thin, which aids quick/efficient gas exchange.	AO1/AO2	1
2e	It reduces the surface area of the alveoli (1) and, therefore, reduces the efficiency of gas exchange (1).	AO1/AO2	2

3a	There is a positive correlation between height and lung volume	AO3	1
3b	180 cm	AO3	1
4a	diaphragm	AO2/AO3	1
4b	It increases the volume (1) inside the bell jar so the air pressure decreases (1) causing the balloon to expand. (For 1 mark, accept air moves into the balloon to fill the extra volume.)	AO2/AO3	2
4c	The balloon would deflate more (1) because the volume inside the bell jar would decrease, causing the air pressure to increase (1).	AO2/AO3	2

Biology – Digestion (core)

Q	Answer	AO	Marks
1	carbohydrates – provide energy fats – provide reserve energy supply and insulation proteins – important for growth and repair (1 mark for one correct line, 2 marks for 3 correct lines.)	AO1	2
2a	C	AO1	1
2b	A	AO1	1
2c	It secretes acid to kill bacteria (1). It contains an enzyme to break down protein (1).	AO1	2
2d	Digestive enzymes break down foods (1). Food is absorbed through the wall of the gut into the blood (1).	AO1	2
2e	large intestine	AO1	1
3	red meat, beans, pulses and green vegetables	AO2	1
4a	5000	AO2/AO3	1
4b	60%	AO2/AO3	1
4c	Because she is likely to consume more than the daily requirement (1). Excess kJ/food consumption will increase her risk of becoming overweight/obese (1).	AO2/AO3	2
5	Enzymes are used to break up larger molecules into smaller ones (1). The small molecules can pass through the intestine wall into the blood (1).	AO1	2

Biology – Digestion (extended)

Q	Answer	AO	Marks

1a	A – stomach (1) B – pancreas (1)	AO1	2
1b	The proteins get further digested into amino acids (1) by protease enzymes (1). (Accept smaller molecules in place of amino acids and accept enzymes in place of protease enzymes.)	AO1	2
1c	They are needed for growth and repair	AO1	1
2	good blood supply – efficiently absorb and carry away the nutrients (1) finger-like shape of villi – increases surface area for absorption of nutrients (1).	AO1	2
3	If the villi are damaged the intestine won't be able to absorb the nutrients from the small intestine. Therefore, the person is likely to lose weight (1).	AO2	1
4	Anaemia is caused by lack of iron (1) and these foods are rich in iron (1).	AO2	2
5a	5000 kJ	AO2/AO3	1
5b	60 % (Allow 60.2%)	AO2/AO3	1
5c	She is likely to consume more than her daily requirement (1). Excess kJ/food consumption will increase her risk of becoming overweight/obese (1).	AO2/AO3	2
6	Because it would not contain the right balance of nutrients (1). It would not have enough vitamins, minerals or water and would have too much carbohydrates/sugars and fats (1).	AO2	2

Respiration (core)

Q	Answer	AO	Marks
1	chemical (1); energy(1)	AO1	2
2a	carbon dioxide	AO1	1
2b	from the food we eat	AO1	1
2c	from the air we breathe in	AO1	1
3	in all cells	AO1	1
4a	temperature	AO2	1
4b	Any one of: the same batch of yeast the same amount of yeast the amount of glucose the same apparatus	AO2	1
4c	Because glucose is a reactant in fermentation	AO2/AO3	1
4d	carbon dioxide	AO2/AO3	1

4e	The higher the temperature the higher the rate of fermentation in the yeast.	AO3	1
5	The glucose in the drink provides glucose to meet the demands of the muscle cells (1), so they can respire to make energy to contract (1).	AO2	2
6a	lactic acid (1)	AO1	1
6b	In a sprint event the athlete cannot take in enough oxygen to meet the demand (1), whereas during a gentle jog the athlete is able to take in enough oxygen for respiration to be aerobic (1).	AO2	2

Biology – Respiration (extended)

Q	Answer	AO	Marks
1	chemical (1); cells (1)	AO1	2
2	to release energy	AO1	1
3a	carbon dioxide	AO1	1
3b	from the food we eat.	AO1	1
3c	because energy is not a substance	AO1	1
4a	*Any one of:* the same batch of yeast the same amount of yeast the amount of glucose the same apparatus duration of time for measuring bubble production	AO2	1
4b	Because glucose is a reactant in fermentation	AO2/AO3	1
4c	ethanol (1) + carbon dioxide (1)	AO2/AO3	2
5	Because there is a build-up of lactic acid in the muscles during the race that needs to be oxidised (1). This causes an 'oxygen debt' that needs to be 'repaid' after the exercise stops, so the athlete continues to breath hard to supply the extra oxygen (1).	AO2	2
6	In test tube A the geminating seeds in air were respiring and, therefore, producing carbon dioxide (1) which turned the indicator solution from red to yellow (1). In tube B the seeds had been killed by heat, so they did not respire and, therefore, did not produce carbon dioxide gas (1), so the indicator did not change colour/stayed red (1).	AO3	4

Biology – Photosynthesis (core)

Q	Answer	AO	Marks

1	light (1); glucose (1)	AO1	2
2	Plants can make their own food	AO1	1
3	carbon dioxide (1); oxygen (1)	AO1	2
4	*Any one of:* for new growth respiration	AO1	1
5	palisade cells are packed with chloroplasts – to absorb light the leaf surfaces contain tiny holes called stomata – to control the movement of gases in and out of the leaf the leaf contains xylem and phloem tubes – to transport water and food (1 mark for one correct line, 2 marks for three correct lines.)	AO1	2
6	Having large leaves provides a large surface area (1), which means the plant can collect more light energy for photosynthesis (1).	AO2	2
7a	distance between the lamp and beaker	AO2	1
7b	use the same piece of pondweed each time Explanation: if you change the pondweed each time you would be changing a variable (1).	AO3	1
7c	Because oxygen is a product of photosynthesis (1) so the faster the rate of photosynthesis, the more bubbles are given off (1).	AO3	2
8	When plants photosynthesise they remove carbon dioxide from the atmosphere and release oxygen (1). When large areas of forest are removed, less carbon dioxide is removed and less oxygen is released, which could alter the atmospheric composition (1).	AO2	2

Biology – Photosynthesis (extended)

Q	Answer	AO	Marks
1	because they can produce their own food using energy from light	AO1	1
2a	carbon dioxide (1), oxygen (1)	AO1	2
3	*Any two of:* growth to make starch for storage for respiration	AO1	2
4	palisade cells are packed with chloroplasts filled with chlorophyll – to absorb light	AO1	2

	the upper and lower leaf surface contain stomata and guard cells – to control the diffusion of gases in and out of the leaf		
	the leaf contains xylem and phloem tubes – to transport water and food		
	1 mark for one correct line, 2 marks for three correct lines.		
5	Giant Aroid plants grow under the rainforest canopy so need to compete for light (1). Having giant leaves gives a large surface area to collect as much sunlight as possible (1).	AO1	2
6a	*Any two of:* use the same pondweed use the same lamp keep liquid/water surrounding the pondweed the same keep the temperature the same	AO2	2
6b	The size of the bubbles may vary. Counting bubbles is a less accurate measurement (1) than measuring the volume of gas which is more accurate (1).	AO3	2
7a	The level of carbon dioxide will increase and the level of oxygen will decrease	AO2	1
7b	Removing trees means less photosynthesis takes place (1) and, therefore, less carbon dioxide is removed from the atmosphere and less oxygen is released by the trees (1).	AO2	2

Biology – Evolution, extinction and biodiversity (core)

Q	Answer	AO	Marks
1	*Any two of:* food water habitat/shelter/space mates	AO1	2
2a	Some had longer and some had shorter necks.	AO2	1
2b	The length of a giraffe's neck was controlled by its genes. – true (1) The offspring of giraffes with longer necks also had longer necks. – true (1) The length of a giraffe's neck could change in its lifetime depending on the environment where it lived. – false (1)	AO2	3
2c	to allow the giraffe to reach leaves high up in trees	AO2	1
2d	adapted (1); reproduce (1); natural selection (1)	AO1/AO2	3
3a	1990	AO3	1
3b	After 1990 there were no observations of the golden toad.	AO3	1

257

3c	change in habitat due to severe weather conditions	AO2/AO3	1
4	gene bank	AO1	1
5	the variety of living things in an ecosystem	AO1	1
6	To ensure we continue to have the sources of food/materials/medicines that we currently get from different species. *or* The more biodiversity there is, the stronger the ecosystem because small changes will have less of an effect on individual food webs.	AO1	1

Biology – Evolution, extinction and biodiversity (extended)

Q	Answer	AO	Marks
1	Charles Darwin	AO1	1
2	adaptation – change in structure or function of an organism to become more suited to an environment variation – the differences that exist between individuals in a population competition – when organisms all need the same resources, which are in short supply (1 mark for one correct line and 2 marks for three correct lines.)	AO1	2
3	fossils	AO1	1
4a	a species that has died out/no longer exists	AO1	1
4b	Between 1990 and 1992 no golden toads were observed.	AO3	1
4c	*Any one of:* change in habitat severe weather conditions increased competition for food/mates/habitat disease natural disaster *Accept other plausible reasons.*	AO2/AO3	1
4d	gene bank/zoos and plant collections/breeding programmes	AO1	1
5	Variation within a species means that some organisms are likely to be well adapted to survive a change.	AO3	1
6	the variety of living things in an ecosystem	AO2/AO3	1
7	To ensure we continue to have the sources of food/materials/medicines that we currently get from different species. *or*	AO1	1

	The more biodiversity there is, the stronger an ecosystem is because small changes will have less of an effect on food webs.		
8a	That the average fur length of the lemmings decreased between 1800 and 2000	AO3	1
8b	The starting population of lemmings would have had variation in fur length (1). Lemmings that had shorter fur would have been better adapted to the warmer climate (1) and were, therefore, more likely to survive and reproduce (1). This resulted in natural selection over time and the average fur length of the lemmings decreased (1).	AO2/AO3	4

Biology – Genes and inheritance (core)

Q	Answer	AO	Marks
1	offspring (1); DNA (1)	AO1	2
2a	A	AO2	1
2b	B	AO2	1
2c	gene	AO2	1
3	Because the egg and sperm cell join in fertilisation (1) to make a new cell/zygote/baby with 46 chromosomes (1).	AO1	2
4	21	AO2	1
5a	1 Veda 2 Jafar	AO2/AO3	1
5b	Because neither of his parents can roll their tongue (1), so they cannot pass the tongue rolling gene to him (1).	AO2/AO3	2
6	Because polydactyly is caused by a gene mutation (1) and so it can be inherited by a child (1).	AO2	2
7a	What is the structure of DNA?	AO2	1
7b	the X-ray photograph	AO2	1
7c	Without the expertise of Franklin and Wilkins in producing an X-ray photograph of DNA, Watson and Crick would not have had the important clues about the structure of DNA (1).	AO2/AO3	1

Biology – Genes and inheritance (extended)

Q	Answer	AO	Marks
1	A chromosome (1) B DNA (1) C gene (1)	AO1	3
2	DNA is only found in egg and sperm cells. – false (1)	AO1	3

	DNA is made from two strands twisted together to make a double helix. – true (1) A gene codes for a particular characteristic. – true (1)		
3a	1 Veda 2 Jafar	AO2/AO3	1
3b	Rab does not have the gene for tongue rolling and neither does his wife (1), so they won't pass on the tongue rolling gene to the child (1).	AO2	2
4	Skin cell – 44 Heart cell – 44 (1) Sex cell – 22 (1)	AO2/AO3	2
5	Because every sperm cell contains a random mix of the father's genetic information and every egg cell contains a random mix of the mother's genetic information (1), so each child inherits a different mixture of genetic information (1).	AO1/AO2	2
6a	What is the structure of DNA?	AO2/AO3	1
6b	1 Franklin's X-ray photograph (1) 2 Chargraff's discovery about bases (1)	AO2/AO3	2

Based on a judgement of the level of demand of each test we would estimate that students who achieve 80% or more on core tests would be on track to achieve a grade 5 at GCSE level and students who achieve 80% of more on extended tests would be on track to achieve a grade 7 or above at GCSE level. Please bear in mind that progress is not always linear and that teachers remain the best judge of student performance. This is for your guidance only.

Chemistry – The Periodic Table (core)

Q	Answer	AO	Marks
1a	E	AO1	1
1b	**B** (1); **C** (1)	AO1	2
1c	hydrogen	AO1	1
1d	Any complete row shaded	AO1	1
2a	iodine	AO2	1
2b	liquid; gas	AO2	1
2c	The boiling point will increase (1) because it will follow the same pattern as the melting point (1).	AO2	2
3a	*Any two of:* In both tables the elements are put in groups. In both tables the elements are placed in order of increasing mass. The early table has some gaps but the modern table does not. The early table has 8 columns but the modern one has a lot more.	AO3	2
3b	Based on his observations and experiments, Mendeleev predicted that some elements were missing (1). He left gaps in the table so that when the missing elements were discovered they could go in the correct place (1).	AO1	2
4a	As you go down the group both melting points and boiling points decrease.	AO2	1
4b	Bar drawn in correct place, in the range 800–1200°C.	AO2	1
4c	Answer in the range 20–35°C.	AO3	1

Chemistry – The Periodic Table (extended)

Q	Answer	AO	Marks
1a	i **A** (1) ii It is in group 0 – the unreactive noble gases (1).	AO1/AO2	2
1b	i **D** (1) ii It is a transition metal; it is not very reactive but does have a large surface area for the gaseous reaction to take place (1).	AO1/AO2	2
1c	Second column from right correctly shaded.	AO1	1
2a	Reactivity increases as you go down the group (1).	AO1	2

Q	Answer	AO	Marks
	Lithium, at the top of the group, fizzed slowly compared to potassium, at the bottom of the group, which fizzed violently (1).		
2b	Sodium reacts with the oxygen in the air.	AO1	1
2c	sodium oxide	AO1	1
2d	The shiny surface would go dull more rapidly than the surface of sodium did.	AO2	1
3a	As you go down the group both melting points and boiling points increase.	AO2	1
3b	A substance is in the liquid state when at a temperature between its melting point and boiling point (1). Bromine melts at –2°C and boils at about 70°C. 20°C is between these values so bromine must be a liquid at 20°C (1).	AO2	2
3c	*Any one of:* It is a solid at room temperature. It has a melting point above that of iodine, in the range 275–325°C. It has a boiling point above that of iodine, in the range 325–375°C.	AO3	1
3d	fluorine + sodium iodide	AO2	1
3e	fluorine + sodium iodide → sodium fluoride + iodine	AO3	1

Chemistry – Materials (core)

Q	Answer	AO	Marks
1a	element (1); molecule (1); compound (1)	AO1	3
2a	Magnesium oxide	AO1	1
2b	*Any one of:* The solution was alkaline. Metal oxides are basic and dissolve in water to produce an alkali.	AO2	1
2c	*Any one of:* The final solution was neutral. The magnesium oxide had neutralised the acid.	AO2	1
2d	magnesium chloride + water	AO2	1
3a	carbon dioxide	AO1	1
3b	CO_2	AO1	1
3c	green; red/orange	AO3	1
4a	A polymer is a very large molecule made from lots of smaller molecules joined together in a repeating pattern.	AO1	1
4b	Cut plastic bags into strips the same size (1). Hang strips onto a clamp and stand (1).	AO3	4 (2 marks for making a list of tasks, full marks for

	Attach weights the same size to plastic strips (1). Measure how much each plastic strip stretches (1). *Or similar method.*		putting list into a logical sequence)
4c	The length and width of the plastic strips *Or any other suitable independent variable.*	AO2	1

Chemistry – Materials (extended)

Q	Answer	AO	Marks
1a	C	AO2	1
1b	B	AO2	1
1c	E	AO2	1
1d	C	AO2	1
1e	Any diatomic molecule, for example, hydrogen, oxygen, nitrogen, chlorine	AO2	1
2a	*Row 1:* CO_2 (1) *Row 2:* magnesium oxide; no; yes (1) *Row 3:* CaO (1) *Row 4:* sulfur dioxide; yes; no (1)	AO1	4
2b	$CaSO_4$ (1); H_2O (1)	AO2	2
3a	*Any well-reasoned answer, for example:* Aluminium is more dense than carbon fibre so an aluminium racquet will feel heavier to the player than a racquet made from carbon fibre. Carbon fibre materials have a higher strength/weight ratio and lower density than aluminium which makes them easier to use as they are very strong but feel light.	AO3	1
3b	Steel (1). It is strong and sturdy, as shown by strength in MPa/will withstand high pressure before breaking (1)	AO2	2
3c	*Any one of:* Plates need to be made of a non-toxic material. Plates need to be made of a chemically stable material.	AO2	1
3d	*Any one of:* Floor tiles need to be hard and resistant to wear. Floor tiles need to be made of a material that is an electrical insulator. Floor tiles need to be made of a material that is a thermal insulator.	AO2	1

Chemistry – Energetics (core)

Q	Answer	AO	Marks
1a	C	AO1	1

1b	exothermic (1); higher (1)	AO1	2
2	Condensing (1) and freezing (1) are exothermic. Melting (1) and evaporating (1) are endothermic	AO2	4
3a	*Top row* +28.2 (1) *Bottom row* −2.2 (1)	AO2	2
3b	Sodium ethanoate and water (1) The increase in temperature will warm your hands (1).	AO3	2
3c	Citric acid and hydrogen sodium carbonate (1) There was a decrease in temperature (1).	AO2	2
4a	... to speed up the reaction without changing the reactants.	AO1	1
4b	A	AO3	1
4c	Gas was produced more quickly in reaction A (no gas was produced in the first 4 minutes of reaction B).	AO3	1

Chemistry – Energetics (extended)

Q	Answer	AO	Marks
1	broken (1); released (1); endothermic (1)	AO1	3
2a	$2MgO$	AO2	2 (1 mark for correct formula, 1 mark for balancing)
2b	*From the top:* $2Mg + O_2$ (1); heat is released (1); $2MgO$ (1)	AO2	3
2c	Bonds between Mg atoms and bonds between atoms in O_2 molecules are broken (1). New bonds between Mg atoms and O atoms are formed (1).	AO2	2
2d	The reactants would have a lower energy than the products (1). The arrow would point up, not down (1).	AO2	2
3a	Endothermic (1). The ice is melting and so is taking in energy from the surroundings (1).	AO3	2
3b	Liquid water is boiling. Molecules are vibrating and gaining enough energy (1) to escape from the liquid state into the gaseous state (1).	AO3	2

Chemistry – Chemical reactions (core)

Q	Answer	AO	Marks
1a	Combustion (1); Oxidation (1)	AO1	2
1b	carbon (1); hydrogen (1); water (1)	AO1	3
1c	They are rearranged to form a new product.	AO2	1
1d	During a chemical reaction atoms cannot be made or destroyed (1) – they only rearrange and form new products (1).	AO1	2

2a	85 g	AO3	1
2b	The law of conservation of mass must be obeyed (1). There are no bubbles to indicate that a gas has been produced, so the mass of the products must be the same as the mass of the reactants (1).	AO2/AO3	2
3a	Oxygen atoms have combined with magnesium atoms to form magnesium oxide (1). All atoms have mass, so magnesium oxide will be heavier than the magnesium at the start (1).	AO3	2
3b	12 + 8 = 20 g	AO2	1
4a	It stayed the same.	AO3	1
4b	No particles could enter or leave the sealed flask.	AO3	1

Chemistry – Chemical reactions (extended)

Q	Answer	AO	Marks
1a	Thermal decomposition	AO1	1
1b	*Any one of:* Wear safety glasses. Put Bunsen burner on a heatproof mat. Support the test tube containing lime water.	AO1	1
1c	*Any one of:* Lime water goes from colourless to cloudy/milky. Green solid turns black.	AO1	1
1d	CO_2	AO2	1
1e	−4.4 (g)	AO2	1
1f	The law of conservation of states that the mass of products must be the same as the mass of reactants (1). One of the products is carbon dioxide gas which has escaped from the test tube (1). Therefore the decrease in the mass of the test tube and its contents is the same as the mass of carbon dioxide formed (1).	AO2/AO3	3
2a	carbon, hydrogen, oxygen	AO1	1 (all three needed for 1 mark)
2b	water (1); carbon dioxide (1)	AO2	2
2c	The ethanol has reacted with oxygen/oxygen has added on to carbon and hydrogen atoms in ethanol.	AO2	1
3a	Mg is the most reactive because it reacts with both $ZnCl_2$ and $CuCl_2$ whereas Zn only reacts with $CuCl_2$ (1). Copper is the least reactive because it does not react with any of the salts (1).	AO3	2 (to achieve full marks the answer must refer to the data in the table)

| 3b | $Mg + CuCl_2 \rightarrow Cu + MgCl_2$ | AO3 | 2 (1 mark for correct reactants, 1 mark for correct products) |

Chemistry – The atmosphere (core)

Q	Answer	AO	Marks
1a	Correctly labelled axes (1). Correctly drawn and labelled bars (2).	AO2	3 (2 marks if all bars are correct, 1 mark if 1 or 2 are incorrect)
1b	nitrogen	AO1	1
1c	N_2	AO1	1
1d	*Any one of:* The amount of water vapour depends on the weather. When it is wet (or dry) there is more (or less) water vapour present. *Or similar suitable answer.*	AO2	1
2a	Diagram correctly labelled. *Left to right:* combustion (1); respiration (1); death (1)	AO1	3
2b	photosynthesis	AO2	1
2c	*Any one of:* When the dog dies or organic waste matter is excreted from the dog, a carbon atom from the dog will be in the decaying organic matter (1). As the decomposing matter respires, the carbon atom will enter the atmosphere as CO_2 (1). The C atom will then enter the tree during photosynthesis (1). During respiration the C atom from the dog becomes CO_2 (1). The dog breathes out CO_2 which enters the atmosphere (1). The C atom then enters the tree during photosynthesis (1). *Or any other correct answer that is based on the diagram.*	AO3	3
2d	*Any one of:* Burning fossil fuels Deforestation	AO2	1
2e	Carbon dioxide is a greenhouse gas (1). Scientists believe that increasing levels of greenhouse gases lead to global warming (1).	AO1	2

Chemistry – The atmosphere (extended)

Q	Answer	AO	Marks
1a	21% – oxygen 78% – nitrogen	AO1	2

1b	*Reasonable answers include:* A bigger population will increase the level of CO_2 in the atmosphere (1) because more fossil fuels will be burned (in cars, in factories, heating homes) (1). A bigger population will increase the level of CO_2 and decrease the amount of O_2 (1) because more people means greater levels of respiration (1). *Accept other suitable answers.*	AO2	2 (1 mark for the impact, 1 mark for the linked reason)
2a	respiration; combustion	AO2	1 (both needed to get 1 mark)
2b	Carbon in atmospheric carbon dioxide is taken in by plants during photosynthesis (1). The carbon is transferred to: animals when the plant is eaten, decaying matter when the plants die, and fossil fuels after millions of years. (1) The carbon is returned to the atmosphere during: respiration of plants, animals or decomposers, and combustion of fossil fuels (1).	AO2	3 (statements should be in a logical order but do not need to include all aspects listed)
3a	From 1000 to 1900 the global temperature was relatively steady, below the 1961–1990 average (1). Since about 1950 there has been a rapid increase to 0.5°C above the 1961–1990 average (1).	AO2	2
3b	Human activities, such as burning fossil fuels, deforestation and increased intensive farming methods (1), have led to an increase in levels of CO_2 and CH_4 in the atmosphere (1). CO_2 and CH_4 are both greenhouse gases (1). Rising temperatures are due to global warming caused by an increase in greenhouse gases (1).	AO2/AO3	4
3c	*Any two of:* Planting more trees to remove CO_2. Use of renewable energy such as solar power or wind power to generate electricity instead of burning fossil fuel. Change farming methods (e.g. reduce reliance on fertilisers, grow crops better suited to actual environment) to reduce production of CO_2. *Accept other suitable answers.*	AO3	2

Chemistry – The Earth's resources (core)

Q	Answer	AO	Marks
1a	recycle – make new materials from old ones reduce – use less to avoid waste reuse – use the object again	AO1	2 (1 mark if 1 or 2 incorrect)
1b	*Reasonable answers include:*	AO2	2

	Putting recycling bins in public places (1) Kerbside collecting of plastic, glass, cardboard, etc. (1) *Accept other suitable answers.*		
1c	Many of the Earth's resources are finite and will run out if humans don't reduce their usage of them.	AO1	1
2a	extracted (1); harder (1); displace (1); electrolysis (1)	AO1	4
2b	lead (1) + carbon dioxide (1)	AO2	2
2c	carbon	AO2	1
2d	The more reactive element (carbon) displaces the less reactive element (lead).	AO2	1
3a	Recycling aluminium uses 96% less energy than extracting it from raw materials (1). This is because aluminium is a reactive metal; to extract aluminium from raw materials involves electrolysis, a method that uses a lot of energy (1).	AO3	2
3b	Reusing saves energy – to reuse a glass bottle you only need to wash it, which uses less energy than recycling it.	AO3	1

Chemistry – The Earth's resources (extended)

Q	Answer	AO	Marks
1a	Gold	AO1	1
1b	Carbon is a reference point/it is placed in the reactivity series because all of the metals beneath it can be extracted from their ores by heating with a carbon source such as coke.	AO1	1
1c	copper – roasting in air iron – blast furnace potassium – electrolysis	AO2	2 (1 mark if only 1 correct)
1d	Mix the nickel ore with carbon/coke (1). Heat the ore to a very high temperature (1). The carbon will displace the nickel metal from the ore (1).	AO3	3
1e	Aluminium is a reactive metal – it is above carbon in the reactivity series so it has to be extracted by electrolysis (1). A lot of energy is required to heat the aluminium ore to high temperatures so that it melts (1). Energy is also needed for the process of electrolysis (1). Electrolysis is also expensive because special electrolysis cells are needed (1).	AO2	4
1f	*Any one of:* Recycling aluminium is cheaper that extracting it from its ore. Recycling aluminium uses less energy than extracting it from its ore.	AO2	1

	Recycling aluminium produces fewer greenhouse gas emissions than extracting it from its ore.		
2a	Approximately twice as much energy is needed to produce 1 kg of HDPE and 1 kg of PP from raw materials as is needed to recycle 1 kg of each plastic (1). For polystyrene more than twice as much energy is needed to produce 1 kg from raw materials than is needed to recycle 1 kg (1). *(Statements should refer to data in table.)*	AO3	2
2b	*Any two of:* Initial costs of setting up recycling centres can be expensive. Recycled products may be of lower quality. Recycling sites can be unsafe/unhygienic. Not all councils provide recycling centres/kerbside services. It can be difficult/time consuming to recycle. *Accept other reasonable answers.*	AO2	2

Based on a judgement of the level of demand of each test we would estimate that students who achieve 80% or more on core tests would be on track to achieve a grade 5 at GCSE level and students who achieve 80% of more on extended tests would be on track to achieve a grade 7 or above at GCSE level. Please bear in mind that progress is not always linear and that teachers remain the best judge of student performance. This is for your guidance only.

Physics – Sound (core)

Q	Answer	AO	Marks
1	**vibration** (1); **longitudinal** (1); **medium** (1)	AO1	3
2	B (1); A (1); D (1)	AO1	3
3	The note middle C on a piano (frequency = 260 Hz) The siren on a police car (frequency = 600 to 900 Hz) The highest note on a cymbal (frequency = 5 kHz) *(2) for all three correct and no other boxes ticked.* *(1) for one or two correct and up to one other box ticked.* *(0) for none, or one or two correct and more than one other box ticked.*	AO2	2
4a	Pile drivers make noises of high amplitude/loudness/volume (1). These high amplitude waves cause the parts of the ear/eardrum to vibrate so much they may be damaged (1).	AO2	2
4b	*Any **one** of:* Use ear defenders/protectors/plugs. Reduce the amount of time spent drilling. *Accept any other sensible suggestion.*	AO3	1
5a	Air is a gas, and in a gas the particles are very far apart so do not collide often/do not transmit/allow waves to pass easily (1). Steel is a solid with atoms arranged in a regular pattern that can collide/vibrate more easily (1).	AO2	2
5b	In contact with the metal rails.	AO3	1
6a	Sound that is at higher frequencies than a human can hear/above 20 kHz (1).	AO2	1
6b	*Any **one** of:* Scanning unborn babies (1). To ease pain; repair soft tissue damage; treat arthritis; physiotherapy (1).	AO3	1

Physics – Sound (extended)

Q	Answer	AO	Marks
1a	A = wavelength (1)	AO1	2

	B = amplitude (1)		
1b	Longitudinal means the wave moves in the same direction as the particles vibrate (1). Medium means the substance the sound wave travels through (1).	AO1	2
2a	The longest wavelength = A (1) The highest frequency = D (1)	AO1	2
2b	1 : 3 (1) *Accept* 2 : 6	AO2	1
3a	frequency (1)	AO1	1
3b	20 Hz to 20 kHz/20 000 Hz (1)	AO2	1
3c	*Any one of:* His ears have been damaged by the work he did (1). As people get older, they can hear a narrower range of frequencies (1).	AO2	1
4a	Air is a gas, and in a gas the particles are very far apart so do not collide often/do not transmit/allow waves to pass easily (1). Steel is a solid with atoms arranged in a regular pattern that can collide/vibrate more easily (1).	AO2	2
4b	Sound requires a medium to travel through/there are no particles for the sound wave to vibrate (1).	AO2	1
4c	Any value or range between 1482 and 5960 m/s (1)	AO3	1
5a	Using a quiet room makes it easier to detect the sounds the student wants to measure/reduces the background noise/makes the measurements more sensitive (1).	AO2	1
5b	An echo/a reflection (1).	AO3	1

Physics – Contact forces, moments and pressure (core)

Q	Answer	AO	Marks
1	$$pressure = \frac{force}{area}$$	AO1	1
2a	*(1) for vertical upwards direction, same or very similar length to weight arrow.*	AO2	1
2b	Two forces are balanced/equal and opposite.	AO1	1

3a	Object in **A** will turn/rotate around the pivot.	AO2	1
3b	3 N (1) to the right (1)	AO2	2
4a	For 300 g, the extension of 3.6 cm is wrong.	AO1	1
4b	Extension = 24.6 – 20.0 = 4.6 (cm)	AO2	1
4c	*(1) for correct data point plotted 300 g, 4.6 cm.* *(1) for good line of best fit.*	AO2	2
4d	Yes	AO3	1
5a	Force due to gravity/their weight.	AO2	1
5b	Opening the parachute means they have/present a larger surface area (perpendicular to) the direction of the fall (1). Air resistance is proportional to/depends upon the surface area, so they experience a greater upwards force of air resistance (1).	AO2	2
5c	Pressure in the air is due to the weight of air above pushing downwards (1). The further they fall, the larger the weight of air above them, so they feel the pressure of the air increasing (1).	AO3	2

Physics – Contact forces, moments and pressure (extended)

Q	Answer	AO	Marks
1	*(1) for weight arrow, from centre or bottom of book, vertically downwards.* *(1) for reaction arrow, vertical upwards direction, same or very similar length to weight arrow.*	AO2	2

2a	Moment = force × (perpendicular) distance to pivot (1) = 8 N × 0.5 m = 4 N m (1) *4 Nm with no working scores (2)*	AO2	2
2b	3 N (1) to the left (1)	AO2	2
3a	For 300 g, the extension of 3.6 cm is wrong.	AO1	1
3b	Extension = 24.6 − 20.0 = 4.6 (cm)	AO2	1
3c	 *(2) for all correct data points plotted including 300 g, 4.6 cm. (±0.5 square).* *(1) if only two or three data points plotted correctly.* *(1) for sensible choice of axes and range.*	AO2	3
3d	*(1) for good line of best fit. (See diagram in answer to 3c.)*	AO2	1
3e	Yes, it does obey Hooke's law (1) because the graph is a straight line through the origin/indicates extension proportional to mass added (1).	AO3	2
4	Pressure in water increases with depth due to the weight of liquid above (1). The further they dive, the forces increase to the point where the pressure on their bodies/lungs would cause injury (1).	AO3	2

Physics – Light (core)

Q	Answer	AO	Marks
1	**True** (1); **False** (1); **True** (1); **False** (1)	AO1	4

2a	 (1) mark for each straight-line reflected ray at a suitable angle (marked by eye).	AO2	2
2b	A	AO2	1
3	The lens focuses the light rays (onto the retina) (1). The image is formed on the retina (1). *Accept other sensible descriptions.*	AO2	2
4	**towards** (1); **slower** (1); **away from** (1); **refraction** (1)	AO1/AO2	4
5	White light passes through colour filters unaffected. **Incorrect** (1) Red light passes through red filters but not through green filters. **Correct** (1) A blue filter is needed to block both green and red light. **Cannot tell** (1) *(Note: the question is clear about using only the evidence provided.)*	AO3	3

Physics – Light (extended)

Q	Answer	AO	Marks
1	Scattering D Specular reflection B Opaque C Translucent E Transparent A (1) for each correct selection	AO1	5
2a	 (1) mark for each straight-line reflected ray at a suitable angle (measured by eye).	AO2	2

2b	Two dotted lines drawn back to the right from the reflected rays added in 2a (1). Image marked where the dotted lines cross, level with the object (1). Image the same distance behind the mirror as the object is in front (1).	AO2	3
3	part **a** – the refracted ray within the block, angled towards the first normal (1). part **b** – the second normal (1). part **c** – the refracted ray to the right of the block, angled away from the second normal, parallel with the incident ray (1).	AO2	3
4a	Red light does not pass through green filters.	AO2	1
4b	A green object (1). Only green light passes through a green filter (1) *or* Green filter blocks all light except green (1).	AO3	2

Physics – Magnetism and electromagnetism (core)

Q	Answer	AO	Marks
1	**non-contact** (1); **two poles** (1); **repel** (1); **attract** (1).	AO1	4
2	Both poles are south poles, so they repel. *and* Both poles are north poles, so they repel. *(1) for both of the above. Do not accept other combinations.*	AO1	1

3a		AO2	1
	(1) for all correct N and S labels (although order can be reversed i.e. reading from left to right, N then S on left magnet, N then S on right magnet).		
3b	*See 3a for diagram. All added arrows point from N to S.*	AO2	1
4	*Any two of:* Use a compass/lodestone/suspended magnet to show that it aligns with the magnetic field of the Earth (1). Aurora/light displays at night caused by charged particles interacting with the Earth's magnetic field (1). The detection of 'stripes' of magnetically aligned rocks in the Earth's crust (1). Living things such as pigeons which use the magnetic field to navigate/change direction (1).	AO1/AO2	2
5	**low/weak**; **weak/low** (1); **high/strong** (1); **high/strong**; **breaks** (1)	AO2	3
6a	Connect the wire to the battery using crocodile clips to make a circuit (1). Move the compass near the wire to show the compass needle deflects/moves (1).	AO2	2
6b	Arrange the wire through a hole in the paper so the wire is at right-angles to the paper (1). Move the compass around the wire and draw or plot on the paper the directions the compass points to (1).	AO3	2

Physics – Magnetism and electromagnetism (extended)

Q	Answer	AO	Marks
1	**non-contact** (1); **electric** (1); **gravitational** (1); **magnetic** (1)	AO1	4

2	*Both pairs of N and S labels added, order left to right S, N, S, N.* *Also accept order left to right N, S, N, S.* *Do not accept N, N, S, S or similar, or S, N, N, S, etc.*	AO2	1
2b	*See 2a for diagram. All added arrows point from N to S.*	AO2	1
3a	Any one of: Hang a bar magnet/magnetised needle from a thread cradle/freely twisting string and allow the magnet to line up with the Earth's magnetic field. Use a magnetic compass and allow it to come to a rest, when it lines up with the Earth's magnetic field.	AO2	1
3b	Magnetic south pole.	AO1	1
4a	Scatter iron filings over the sheet of paper.	AO2	1
4b	*Lines are continuous and smoothly curved, except those that go towards left or right edge, where there is not enough space to show the full loops (1).* *Loops are getting gradually further apart moving away from the central axis of the coil (1).* *Arrows are all pointing from N to S (1).*	AO2	3
5a	With the circuit switched on, the electromagnet produces a magnetic field that attracts iron and steel objects and holds them to the magnet as it is moved around on a crane (1). When the object is in position, the circuit is switched off, the magnetic field is off and the object is dropped (1).	AO2	2

Q	Answer	AO	Marks
5b	Increasing the current in the coil/potential difference across the coil/voltage of the power supply (1). Increasing the number of coils in the wire (1).	AO3	2

Physics – Energy: work done, heating and cooling (core)

Q	Answer	AO	Marks
1	work done – Energy is transferred to an object when it is pushed along a floor. conduction – Energy is transferred by particles vibrating in a solid. convection – Energy is transferred by hot water rising and cold water sinking, causing circulation. radiation – Energy is transferred by infrared waves.	AO1	4
2	**force** (1) × **distance moved** (1) **remains constant** (1); **force** (1); **doubled** (1)	AO1/AO2	5
3a	A liquid warming up, then boiling to become a gas, then warming up more (1).	AO2	1
3b	The particles become further apart and move faster/speed up (1).	AO2	1
4	*Any three of:* The silvered surfaces reflect energy and reduce radiation (1). A vacuum contains no particles, so it reduces conduction (1). The stopper stops the air above the liquid mixing with the air outside, reducing convection (1). The stopper keeps gas particles from moving outside, reducing evaporation (1). The stopper is made of an insulator, reducing conduction (1).	AO2	3
5a	Energy is transferred from a hotter to a colder place.	AO3	1
5b	We could investigate: the rate at which the tea transfers energy by measuring its temperature at different times.	AO3	1

Physics – Energy: work done, heating and cooling (extended)

Q	Answer	AO	Marks
1	Convection is the transfer of energy (1) caused by the movement of particles (in a liquid or gas)/circulation of particles in a liquid or gas where hotter areas tend to rise and cooler areas tend to sink (1).	AO1	2
2	Conduction: **medium**; Radiation: **no medium**; Convection: **medium**	AO1	3

	(1) for each of the above		
3a	Work done = 5000 N × 0.20 m = 1000 (1) N m (1)	AO2	2
3b	Conservation of energy means work done is the same, so 500 N × distance = 1000 N m (1) Distance = 2.0 m (1) *Also accept a correct calculation based on an incorrect answer from 3a.*	AO2	2
3c	*Any two of:* Energy transferred in the muscles/body of the mechanic (e.g. heat from the effort needed) (1). Energy transferred as heat to the surroundings (1). Energy stored in stretching/compression of the materials in the jack (1). *Accept any other sensible suggestion (1).*	AO3	2
4a	Energy is transferred from a hotter to a colder place (1).	AO2	1
4b	*Any two of:* Insulate the cup to reduce energy lost as heat to the surroundings (1). Put a lid on the cup to reduce convection/evaporation (1). Place the whole apparatus in a silvered box to reduce radiation out/in (1). *Accept any other sensible suggestion (1).*	AO2	2
4c	*Any sensible and scientifically expressed question involving a variable (1) with some suggestion of method or means or effect (1).* *Examples include:* Investigate whether changing the starting temperature (1) affects the rate of energy transfer (1). Investigate how changing the volume (or surface area) of tea (1) affects the rate of energy transfer (1).	AO3	2

Physics – Waves: properties and effects (core)

Q	Answer			AO	Marks
1	Echo			AO1	1
2	**a** Type of wave	Speed of wave in air (m/s)	**b** Transverse or longitudinal	AO1	4
	light (1)	300 000 000	transverse (1)		
	sound (1)	330	longitudinal (1)		
3a	Infrared			AO1	1
3b	Ultraviolet			AO1	1

3c	Ultraviolet/B	AO2	1
3d	Ultraviolet waves transfer energy to the skin and can cause sunburn and skin cancer (1) so suntan lotion blocks/reduces the amount/intensity of these waves reaching the skin (1).	AO2	2
4a	They are reflected.	AO2	1
4b	*Waves should be reflected at an approximately correct angle (i.e. same angle to the other side of the normal to the barrier) (1) and be straight, with the distance between the reflected wavefronts the same as the incident wave fronts (1).*	AO2	2
5a	*A single wave with approximately double the amplitude and the same wavelength of the two original waves (1).*	AO2	1
5b	The waves will cancel out (1) so the resultant wave will be a flat/straight line (1).	AO3	2

Physics – Waves: properties and effects (extended)

Q	Answer	AO	Marks
1	transverse (1); longitudinal (1); transverse (1)	AO1	3
2	Transverse waves vibrate/oscillate from side to side/at right angles to the direction of travel of the wave (1). Longitudinal waves vibrate/oscillate along the direction of travel of the wave (1).	AO2	2
3		AO2	1

	A single wave with approximately double the amplitude and the same wavelength of the two original waves.		
4	**frequency** (1); **loudspeaker** (1); **microphone** (1); **distance** (1); **time** (1)	AO2	5
5a	Time = 0.007 – 0.001 = 0.006 (1) seconds	AO2	1
5b	$speed = \dfrac{distance}{time} = \dfrac{2.0}{0.006}$ = 330 m/s (to 2 significant figures) *Accept 333 m/s or 333.3 m/s*	AO2	2
5c	Repeat the experiment to take at least three values (1) then calculate an average (1). *Also accept suggestions that improve the accuracy of the measurements taken e.g. improved detail visible on the oscilloscope (1) with a description of the effect of the improvement (1).*	AO3	2

Name _____   Class _____

KS3 Science Progress Tests Record Sheet

Biology tests	Mark	Total marks	% score
Organisms: Skeletal and muscular systems		16	
Organisms: Cells to systems		16	
Ecosystems and habitats		16	
Plant reproduction		16	
Variation		16	
Human reproduction		16	
Breathing and gas exchange		16	
Digestion		16	
Respiration		16	
Photosynthesis		16	
Evolution, extinction and biodiversity		16	
Genes and inheritance		16	

Chemistry tests	Mark	Total marks	% score
The particulate nature of matter		16	
Pure and impure substances		16	
Acids and alkalis		16	
Chemical reactions of metals and non-metals		16	
Earth and rocks		16	
The Earth in Space		16	
The periodic table		16	
Materials		16	
Energetics		16	
Chemical reactions		16	
The atmosphere		16	
The Earth's Resources		16	

Physics tests	Mark	Total marks	% score
Movement: speed and acceleration		16	
Forces and gravity		16	
Electric circuits: current, potential difference and resistance		16	
Static Electricity		16	
Energy: foods, fuels, power and costs		16	
Energy: transfers		16	
Sound		16	
Contact forces, moments and pressure		16	
Light		16	
Magnetism and electromagnetism		16	
Energy: work done, heating and cooling		16	
Waves: properties and effects		16	
Movement: speed and acceleration		16	

Printed in the USA
CPSIA information can be obtained
at www.ICGtesting.com
LVHW082131161023
761258LV00045B/903

9 780008 333690